EA

FOR MORGAN A. WIDER

AND THE WORTHY WARDROBE

"Through her words and her actions, Morgan offers every person she interacts with a gift—and that gift is letting you know that you are seen. Beyond encouraging you to embrace your unique sense of style unapologetically, and giving thoughtful insight on how to develop that style, Morgan knows how to help you be confident in who you be. And truly, what greater gift is there than that?"

—Elayne Fluker, Author of Get Over 'I Got It!' and
Host of the "Support is Sexy" Podcast

"Morgan shows up in the world as a positive, encouraging voice and is in the change business! Not just changing clothes and body perceptions but changing the world."

—Jennifer Davis, Head of Product Marketing,
AWS Training and Certification, Amazon

"Morgan is a true professional with a passion to share what being a 'stylish' woman means to all women. The most valued service she provides to the women we work with is how she always models what a smart, successful woman should look like, sound like, and act like."

—Susan Bonds-McCulloch, Executive
Director, Dress for Success-Atlanta

"*The Worthy Wardrobe* is not your typical wardrobe or style book. Through her profound insights, practical advice, and often amusing storytelling, Morgan helps us see how our wardrobes are not just a bunch of clothes, but rather a reflection of who we are and how we truly feel about ourselves."

—**Kailei Carr, Host of the "Beyond the Business Suit" Podcast and CEO of The Asbury Group**

"Morgan dishes out incredibly helpful wardrobe and professional style advice, using personal accounts infused with grace and humor to make you feel an immediate kinship with her. Her perspective pushed me to look at my wardrobe through a fresh lens, imbuing a self-confidence that allowed me to part ways with clothes that were no longer serving me."

—**Marissa Paulson, Divisional Merchandise Planning, Target**

"For once there is a book that explores the adoration women have for style and fashion, while tackling the even more pressing concerns of body consciousness and societal pressure imposed by what we wear. Morgan provides the quintessential balance of helping you engage in honest ideas about self-discovery, being vulnerable, and building you up to stand before a mirror and have real love for the reflection you see."

—**Montrice Perry, Wealth Advisor**

THE WORTHY
WARDROBE

THE WORTHY WARDROBE

YOUR GUIDE TO STYLE, SHOPPING & SOUL

MORGAN A. WIDER

NEW DEGREE PRESS

COPYRIGHT © 2020 MORGAN A. WIDER

All rights reserved.

THE WORTHY WARDROBE

Your Guide to Style, Shopping & Soul

ISBN   978-1-64137-966-3   *Paperback*

            978-1-64137-794-2   *Kindle Ebook*

            978-1-64137-795-9   *Ebook*

I dedicate this book to you.
May you find peace within yourself and within your closet.

CONTENTS

———

AUTHOR'S NOTE   13

INTRODUCTION   15

PART 1:   **PERFECT**   **25**

CHAPTER 1:   MY STORY   27

CHAPTER 2:   GOLDEN   45

CHAPTER 3:   FOUNDATION   53

CHAPTER 4:   FAIRY GODMOTHER   67

CHAPTER 5:   BODY LOVE   85

PART 2:   **PRETTY AND PROFESSIONAL**   **103**

CHAPTER 6:   PINK AND BLUE   105

CHAPTER 7:   THE HERO'S JOURNEY   117

CHAPTER 8:   SEXY   133

PART 3:   **PLENTY**   **151**

CHAPTER 9:   LET GO   153

CHAPTER 10:   CLEANING OUT THE CLOSET   165

CHAPTER 11:   STOP SETTLING   181

CHAPTER 12:   INTENTIONAL INVESTING   195

PART 4:   POWERFUL   207

CHAPTER 13: THE POWER WITHIN   209

EPILOGUE: DO THIS FOR YOUR DAUGHTER   215

             SOURCES OF INSPIRATION   217

             ACKNOWLEDGMENTS   225

             APPENDIX   229

"My mission in life is not merely to survive, but to thrive; and to do so with some passion, some compassion, some humor, and some style."

— MAYA ANGELOU

AUTHOR'S NOTE

———

I thought I was just writing "a book," a product to sell after my speaking engagements. I figured I'd expand upon my usual topic of personal branding, wrap it up with some shopping tips, and call it a day.

Turns out, I was writing my healing into existence. As I wrote this "style guide," I began to heal myself from feelings of being invisible, inadequate, and unworthy. *The Worthy Wardrobe* has become my love letter to my former and current selves: to the little girl who felt excluded on the playground; to the teenager without a prom date; to the twenty-nine-year-old who didn't know how to answer the boyfriend who always asked, "What is wrong with you?"; to the thirty-two-year-old jumping from job to job, hoping that maybe one of them wouldn't be "all that miserable"; to the current thirty-six-year-old with more questions than answers.

This book is also a love letter to you. As a wardrobe stylist, I've gotten up close and personal while in the closets of many women, hearing countless stories of tribulations and triumphs. And while the plotlines differ, the lesson is always the same.

We're all on a journey to become the women we were born to be. We don't desire to just *look* like we're worthy of being seen and being loved. We yearn to *know* and experience that worthiness in the depths of our soul.

Writing this book reminded me of that and helped me learn to finally love myself completely. I hope reading it does the same for you.

Yours in Style, Shopping, and Soul,

Morgan

INTRODUCTION

———

I've never met a woman as invisible and forgettable as Dana.

As a stylist, I've met many women. And part of what makes me great at my job is that I'm excellent at remembering not only names and faces, but also what a woman was wearing when we met. But Dana was an exception to the rule.

When I started writing this book, I posted on social media a request to interview women about their wardrobes. I was overwhelmed and extremely grateful that over seventy women from across the country, many of them complete strangers, volunteered to speak with me. Dana was one of those women. At the beginning of our phone interview, she informed me that we met at a women's leadership retreat a few months earlier. To this day, I don't remember us ever crossing paths.

At this retreat, there had been symbolic burnings of what no longer served us, recognition of our core values, tight hugs and hand holding, and lots and lots of tears. Our tears were filled with grief for the women we used to be and joy for the women we were becoming. So when Dana said she had left that place a changed woman, I believed her. Yet I was shocked by her total metamorphic journey.

The Dana who had shown up to that wooded lakeside compound for the retreat was a forty-one-year-old looking for a change. As a VP of banking technology at one of the world's largest banks, Dana was a hard worker and had become the critical resource her team and her family relied on. Because she was always doing things for others, Dana never bothered to care about her image, adopting an invisible wardrobe of baggy black pants, tops, and sweaters.

"I was moving in this invisible state," Dana explained when asked about her wardrobe choices. "I know people physically saw me because they were not bumping into me, but I don't think people *saw* me. Because of that, I thought it didn't matter what I was wearing."

Putting everyone else's needs before her own was becoming a heavy burden. "I felt stuck," recalls Dana. "I was consumed with this feeling of heaviness in my soul that I couldn't break free from. That is why I signed up for the retreat."

While sitting in a crowded conference room surrounded by forty other women, Dana got her breakthrough. An intuitive healer guided Dana into a deep meditation that took her back to her childhood. She was transported to her poor, rural home in Alabama where, as an eager-to-please seven-year-old, she had already assumed the role of servant for her family. While in her trance, she heard her grandmother calling her name "Daaaaannnnnnnnaaaaa" acknowledging her only when it was time to feed the pigs, clean up the horse poop in the yard, or mow the lawn.

"That was when I first began to feel invisible," Dana confided in me. "Despite having three older brothers, I was the one doing all the chores. My grandmother and everyone else only noticed me when they wanted me to do something for them."

While Dana was sitting in that conference room, she felt a heightened sense of power come from her heart. As this feeling grew stronger, her heart beat faster and the tears started streaming down her face. She finally saw that the little girl inside of her was worth more than just being a servant. Her purpose was greater than solely being at the beck and call of everyone else.

BECOMING VISIBLE

"That was literally the moment where I was able to start giving myself permission to show up," she told me, excitement and power in her voice. "I chose to become visible and I knew the first thing I needed to do was change my wardrobe. When I got home, I ordered six dresses from Macy's in my real size."

"Real size? What had you always been wearing?" I asked.

"My real size is a size four," Dana confessed. "I had been wearing a size ten in all of my black clothes because I didn't want anyone to notice me. I admired a more senior female executive who wore sharp skinny pants and dramatic bold blazers. But I never thought that could be me. But when I put on the first dress, a blue Calvin Klein shift with a top-to-bottom zipper, I said to myself, 'Girl, you've been hiding this shape all these years?' I had also ordered a couple of pairs of stilettos and I put a pair on and, instantly, I felt *tall*. I didn't feel small anymore. I felt confident."

Once Dana saw how good she looked in those first six dresses, she ordered six more. Suddenly, her closet was filled with size four dresses . . . and the size ten black drabs are now nowhere to be found.

Now that Dana finally sees herself for more than her professional skills or acts of service, everyone else does too. "I've noticed that, in these dresses, people are talking to me much more—not just about what I can do for them, but just to talk and connect," she proudly shares. "Before, they would just show up when they wanted something from me and leave. But now, 80 percent of those interactions is because they just want to be in my space. I'm attracting so many different kinds of people and opportunities than I ever did before, all thanks to those dresses."

While I will probably never remember the Dana I met at that conference, I will now never forget this story of how clothes are an outer reflection of our inner state.

FORGETTING IN ORDER TO REMEMBER

Spiritual teacher H. Emilie Cady advises that the primary cause of our suffering is being unaware or forgetting that we are spiritual beings. This forgetting causes us to think, feel, speak, and act contrary to our true nature.[1] In Dana's case, her suffering was caused by her forgetting (or maybe never even realizing) that she was worth more than just being a servant to the people in her life.

As women, we are expected to be so many things: professional, hard-working, giving, nurturing, feminine, strong—the list is endless. Determining what all those adjectives mean and look like for us can be exhausting. In both professional and spiritual spheres, we're told that clothes don't matter, that it's more noble to focus on intellect or spiritual connection than our appearance. If you're anything like me or Dana, you have been caught in this twisted web of expectations to look the part of a successful, professional woman but to also be too pious or intelligent to care "*that* much" about your image, while also constantly being judged on your image.

We begin to craft this mold of ourselves, layering on beliefs and expectations that often aren't even our own. Some of us get consumed with chasing perfection, but many of us choose to opt out of personal style, denying its relevance. But by rejecting the outer reflection of ourselves, we reject our inner selves as well and suffer the consequences. Eventually, that stone facade of indifference begins to crack, causing us pain, grief, frustration, and uncertainty about what's ahead.

It's a process of first forgetting who we created ourselves to be, in order to remember who we were meant to be.

---

1   H. Emilie Cady, *Lessons in Truth: A Course of Twelve Lessons in Practical Christianity* (Kansas City: Unity School of Christianity, 1919).

REMEMBERING WHO YOU ARE

This quest for remembering is our spiritual journey, and whether we realize it or not, we're all on one. Deep down, we're being called to discover our true purpose, find fulfillment, and remember who we truly are and why we're here. In my own experience, the first step in that journey was recognizing that my worth extended beyond a job title or relationship status.

For most of my life, I questioned everything about my existence. I never quite felt like I belonged, nor did I ever feel comfortable with being seen. I longed for the answers I assumed everyone else knew. I went searching in all the "conventional" ways: retreats, therapists, coaches, churches, new jobs, new cities, food, wine, and exercise. But it wasn't until I had to pack for a trip to Italy that my transformation truly started.

During the darkest phase of my life, I was working in a job I hated in a brand-new city while living with a brand-new boyfriend. Looking back on it now, I clearly see that the fog I was in, was depression. The long hours at work and the emotional eating resulted in thirty extra pounds and being unable to show up fully for myself or for the relationship.

When a chance to go to Italy for two hundred dollars presented itself to the two of us, I started shopping for new clothes. I refused to wear my daily uniform of too-tight jeans and baggy sweaters to one of the world's most fashionable places. Getting ready for that trip was the fresh start my wardrobe (and my life) needed.

I realize how silly it sounds to say that a shopping spree saved my life, but it's true. After that trip, everything fell apart to fall into place. I finally began to remember who I truly am.

After my own transformative experience and transitioning to my current work as a trusted wardrobe stylist to hundreds of women, I have learned firsthand that the right wardrobe makes life so much easier. Yes, cleaning out their closets and taking them shopping helps solve "Morning Outfit Drama." But this work is more than that.

Styling women is about helping them remember who they are, not the titles they wear: mother, wife, vice president, doctor, middle-aged, or retiree. Or their self-imposed limitations of being too old, too fat, too skinny, too shy, too conservative, or too boring.

With each client, I remember the exact moment she looked at herself in the mirror in her new clothes and saw her *true* self, the self beyond the internal baggage. This is the moment she started to see her own inherent beauty. A light switch gets flipped on and nothing is ever the same for her. As counterintuitive as it seems, clothes are cheaper and quicker than therapy.

HONOR YOUR SOUL

This book is meant to help you build a wardrobe that honors your soul. I'll explore how what we wear reflects our sense of worthiness, as our outer image is merely the result of our thoughts and feelings about ourselves. We'll unpack the baggage that attacks our self-worth and lots of the fears:

- The fear of standing out and being seen.
- Our fears and insecurities about our bodies.
- The fear of failing in our careers.
- The fear of forging a new identity.
- The inability to let go of who we used to be.

I'll be sharing more of my story and the stories of the women I've worked with as evidence that style is definitely a process and not a birthright. If you've ever walked into your jam-packed closet and couldn't find a single thing to wear, you're not alone. If you've ever told yourself you're not buying new clothes until you lose weight, you're not alone either.

This book isn't about "the top ten items" every woman should own. I don't believe in a one-size-fits-all approach to style. Instead, my goal is to help you think differently about yourself; to remind you that you're pretty and perfect just as you are; and that you're on this earth for a purpose. Once that light switch is turned on, you'll feel empowered to make your own decisions about your style.

My suggested wardrobe practices are not another set of rules but, instead, a collection of Truths I've uncovered throughout my own spiritual journey and fifteen years of working in the retail industry. At the end of each chapter are suggestions for you to try and Worthy Words of affirmation to quiet those limiting beliefs in your head.

Will this book solve your childhood trauma? No. Please continue seeing your therapist for that. Am I advocating accruing credit card debt all in the name of fleeting "retail therapy?" Hell no! I've been there, done that, and am still paying for those stupid decisions.

My prayer is this book will inspire you to allow your wardrobe to showcase the worthiness you've realized through the therapy, coaching, self-help books, church, or travel. And if you haven't gotten all the way there yet, that's okay too. Continue to do the work needed to feed your soul. But while you're working on your inner self, don't forget to work on your outer self as well. You're a whole being, with a spirit, mind, and body. All three deserve attention.

Sometimes the inner "a-ha!" moments motivate the change for your outer expression, like Dana's retreat experience. Or sometimes a change in wardrobe, like my Italy packing experience, accelerates the inner work. Neither is better or holier or deeper than the other. It doesn't matter how you get to the well; all that matters is that you drink from it.

By building a wardrobe that matches your truest self, you'll be motivated to do more, try more, explore more, write more, pray more. Your confidence will become contagious and intoxicating. And like Dana, you'll start attracting more goodness into your life.

People will see confidence radiating from within you and want to experience it for themselves. Your self-acceptance and joy will inspire others to show up differently. All of this will certainly lead to new opportunities. Whether it's your career, your love life, your friendships, or yourself, new doors will start opening for you.

Whatever you long to be, or do, or have, you're worthy of it. Now let's get you a wardrobe that reflects that.

PART ONE:

PERFECT

CHAPTER 1

MY STORY

—

Let's just get this out of the way right now. Contrary to what you might think, I was never voted "Best Dressed" in high school.

In fact, I have always felt like "The Other." An outsider. One who doesn't belong.

Growing up in suburban St. Paul, Minnesota, not only was I the tallest kid in class, but I was often the only black girl. By third grade, I had developed hips that mirrored my mother's, which was faster than anyone else in my elementary school. Blending in was literally impossible. Instead, I tried to hide the many things I thought were "wrong" about my body under baggy cargo shorts and striped tee shirts from the boy's husky department.

As the daughter of a woman who had been voted "Best Dressed," my weekends always included mother-daughter trips to T.J. Maxx. Some of my most vivid early childhood memories are of playing inside the racks of clothes and trying on high-heel shoes when my mom wasn't watching.

A CLOSETED CLOTHES LOVER

Some kids spent their weekends at Little League. I spent mine at the mall. I loved watching my mother try on dress after dress. Her joy and appreciation for well-made clothes was infectious and was rooted in her rural upbringing that forced her to wear lots of homemade hand-me-downs.

Determined to give me a different childhood than hers, she filled my closet with miniature versions of her frilly dresses, many of which I hated. Epic showdowns occurred for every special occasion: dress versus jeans; mother versus daughter. Of course, Mom always won.

Yet, despite my tomboy stubbornness, I became a Closeted Clothes Lover at a very early age. While I appreciated a beautiful garment, I didn't feel confident enough to wear anything other than those huskies.

The tomboy plan worked well until junior high. By seventh grade, my hips and butt were fully developed. I was standing eye-to-eye with my teachers and towering over my peers. Amid our middle school angst, clothes became status symbols and indicators of popularity.

One weekend, my mom and I went to the brand-new Mall of America, which, at the time, was the largest mall in the US. Excited and hopeful, we walked into the store 5-7-9. I instantly fell in love with the flared jeans, flannel shirts, and strappy tops. But my infatuation soon turned into confusion. I couldn't find my size of thirteen anywhere in the store. The nonchalant teenage store associate stood idly in the back of the store, refusing to provide any level of customer service. After anxiously examining rack after rack, we walked out. As I looked back at the store entrance, it dawned on me that "5-7-9" wasn't just the store name but also their sizing strategy.

The feeling of rejection hit hard. We walked around the mall some more, but my head hung low. Despite that mall having almost every store imaginable, we found nothing that satisfied my desire to dress like "the cute white girls" from school and TV while still satisfying my mother's idea of coverage and appropriateness.

> I need to see my own beauty and to continue to be reminded that I am enough, that I am worthy of love without effort, that I am beautiful, that the texture of my hair and that the shape of my curves, the size of my lips, the color of my skin, and the feelings that I have are all worthy and okay.
>
> – TRACEE ELLIS ROSS

COVERING UP

This push-pull between my desired image and my mother's demands came to a head after a Saturday morning visit to the hair salon. I had just recently been allowed to straighten my head full of thick, long hair, a far more "grown-up" style compared to the box braids my mother had favored for their convenience. Thanks to the relaxer I got that morning, my hair flowed halfway down my back. I walked into that salon a thirteen-year-old kid, and—despite my baggy jeans, white tank top, plaid shirt tied around my waist, and chunky Doc Marten boots—I left feeling like Naomi Campbell, as the wind blew my hair behind me (this was before Queen Beyoncé ruled the hair toss).

On the way home, we stopped at Burger King for lunch. As my mom picked up our order, I went to the bathroom. As I made my way back to our booth, hair blowing in the wind, I sensed other diners watching me. Before I could even process the joy of that Burger King catwalk, I heard my mother yell across the restaurant, "Morgan! Cover up!"

Once I got to the booth, she insisted I take the plaid shirt off my waist and put it on top of my tank top. What she later recalled as panic for a little girl growing up before her very eyes, I interpreted as censure. The glimmer of attention was now something to be ashamed of, something I should avoid at all costs. My image and body were once again causing unwanted problems and challenges for me.

It didn't feel like it at the time, but I was not at all alone in my body dissatisfaction. According to a 2001 study, girls who perceived themselves to be overweight prior to puberty scored significantly higher on measures of disordered eating, body dissatisfaction, asceticism (severe self-discipline), drive for thinness, impulse regulation, and perfectionism.[2]

While I never developed an eating disorder, the other symptoms are spot-on for the girl I was. I am still working on handling many of these things, especially the perfectionism. Body dissatisfaction is real, and it looks different for different women.

Let go of who you think you're supposed to be; embrace who you are.

−DR. BRENÉ BROWN

Some of us grew up in a household and culture that instilled in us that thin is beautiful. Others were taught that femininity equates to flaunting curves. Some women were raised on old-fashioned country cooking that caused unwanted weight gain, and other women grew up in poverty and never hit puberty correctly because of a lack in adequate nutrients. Some women want to be smaller, while some women want to be bigger.

Even though each of us are beautiful in our own way, the grass always seems to be greener on someone else's lawn.

---

2   Diann M. Ackard, "Association between Puberty and Disordered Eating, Body Image, and Other Psychological Variables," *International Journal of Eating Disorders* 29, no. 2 (2001): 187-194.

A DAZZLING MOMENT

I had my first lesson in appreciating my own body during my freshman year at Georgetown University. Christine and I were in the same dorm and instantly connected over our love of clothes, albeit my love was still a closeted one. Christine, a stunning black Puerto Rican, was from Queens, New York and oozed the urban sex appeal I longed to have. All her tops had a matching belt and shoes. Everything was always fitted and "fresh." She, too, loved exploring our nation's capital by its malls instead of monuments, so we became close friends and shopping buddies.

During one particular trip, we were in line at Express. While I was waiting to purchase my usual jeans and turtleneck sweaters, I saw a light-washed denim mini-skirt with rhinestones on it (it was the 2000s. Bedazzling was a thing). As I stared at the skirt, I longingly sighed and said, "Ugh, that skirt is so cute. I wish I could wear that."

Christine's response shocked me: "Morgan, if I had your shape, I would *totally* wear that."

The silence in that moment was deafening for me. My brain instantly went into overdrive: *Wait, what? Who would ever want* my *shape?* It was unfathomable that the body I had literally been hiding my *entire* life was desirable by someone else. And not just anybody else, but someone whose big boobs I always considered greener grass.

Of course, there was nothing left to do but to actually try on said skirt. We got out of line (God bless you, Christine) and I pulled the skirt in a size ten and a size twelve. Back in the fitting room, I took off my jeans and reached for the size twelve. "Nice try," said Christine, calling me out on my bullshit as only a friend could do. "This miniskirt is not supposed to be loose. Put on that ten."

Caught red-handed in my bagginess addiction, I reluctantly shimmied into the size ten mini skirt. Whoa. My thighs had never seen the light of day like this. My mother's command to "cover up" rang through my ears. But Christine's cheers of approval drowned her out.

"See?" she exclaimed. "I told you that would look amazing on you."

As I stared at this stranger in a bedazzled skirt in the mirror, the volume of Mom's voice in my head lowered. I started to see beauty I didn't know existed.

Each individual woman's body demands to be accepted on its own terms.

–GLORIA STEINEM

I wish I could say, "That skirt came back to my dorm room with me, and I wore it every day during freshman year." But that wouldn't be true. I wasn't quite ready to go from sweatpants to rhinestones on my derriere. However, that fitting room moment was part of my freshman orientation. I began to see that beauty truly does come in all shapes and sizes, even my own, and I gave myself a little more permission to have some fun. I even bought a few pairs of smaller-sized sweatpants.

Sweatpants and boy clothes were my "mumu"—the thing your grandma wears because it's loose and comfortable. Those sweatpants were my safety net, my hideaway, and my way of concealing the body I had always struggled with.

A study of female shoppers examined the relationship between body image and clothing functionality. The results match what I had spent the first twenty-two years of my life doing. The study showed that higher body weight and higher body dissatisfaction rates were related to clothing being used for camouflage rather than for fashion or individuality.[3] This cycle of camouflaging my body and blending into my surroundings was my hamster wheel, repeating itself with different mumus.

A LIFE THAT NO LONGER FIT

In 2006, degree in hand, I headed to San Francisco and the corporate offices of The Gap to put to work my latent love of clothes. During my time working in merchandising with the family of brands that include The Gap, Banana Republic, and Old Navy, I finally quit the mumus. Instead, I took full advantage of my generous employee discount. Jeans from Old Navy, blouses from The Gap, and flats from Banana Republic were my uniform as I moved up the middle-management ranks.

---

3   Marika Tiggemann, "Shopping for Clothes: Body Satisfaction, Appearance Investment, and Functions of Clothing among Female Shoppers," *Body Image* 6, no. 4 (2009): 285-291.

After a few years of being on the opposite side of the country, away from all my family and friends, I was ready to head back East. I moved to New York City, where I spent a few years frolicking with my closest girlfriends, pretending to be the cast of *Sex in the City*. With a new city and a more active social life, my style evolved to fitted dresses, perfect for our Wednesday-night happy hours, which turned into Thursday-morning struggles. The fun of the city didn't last long for me, as two years later, a new job, my parents' relocation, and a new relationship took me to Atlanta.

During the first hour of the first day of that new job, I knew this next phase of my life would be a challenge. The job and boss I had signed on for had changed by the time I arrived. The boyfriend I had fallen hard for while dating long distance wasn't who I thought he was (surprise, surprise). Between a horrible new job and adjusting to living with a man I barely knew, I was miserable.

To add insult to injury, the office where I spent twelve-hour days was across the street from Chick-fil-A. This was the first time I had ever lived in the same city as the holy grail of fast food. I took full advantage, having fried chicken for breakfast, lunch, and even sometimes dinner. On the nights I did make it home to the emotionally distant boyfriend, we both were too tired to cook, so we ordered in or ate heavy meals out. I was literally numbing my feelings with food.

In those first six months, I gained thirty pounds, contributing to what I know now was a deep case of depression. I had lost myself inside of an awful job I didn't understand

and a failing relationship. My weight gain was an outward reflection of a life I no longer had control over.

Every morning, I dreaded getting out of bed. When I finally got up at the last possible minute, I went to my side of the closet and was confronted by the clothes from my New York City life that no longer fit. Being reminded of the past and feeling like a total failure was the worst possible way to start each day. Those dresses in bold prints and bright colors represented a life that no longer belonged to me. The only solution I had the mental capacity for was squeezing into too-tight jeans and borrowing a sweater or shirt from his side of the closet. The mumus were back.

As soon as I got to work, I would numb that awful feeling with a chicken biscuit. That vicious cycle of "Morning Outfit Drama" and fried chicken went on for a full year. I barely existed. I was always sick with a cold or flu. I would blow up at the smallest conflict. I got my first ever bad performance review. I was truly miserable.

WAITING FOR "THE DAY"

For some women, this would have been a motivator to eat better, join a gym, and make whatever changes were necessary to get back control of their life. In my depressed state, I went into denial. At first, it was the denial that I looked "*that* bad" and denial that this lifeless existence was "*that* awful." Then came the regret and the guilt: *I shouldn't have eaten that chicken biscuit. I'm such a failure.* This turned into the shame of not feeling worthy of new clothes.

Whether it's too-tight pants or sweaters from the men's department, I've seen many women over the years bear those same cloaks of shame.

I kept waiting for "The Day." The day chicken biscuits stopped tasting so delicious. The day I finally said "enough" and left work in time to make a CrossFit class. The day my boyfriend told me I looked beautiful. Those days never came. But what did come was a two-hundred-dollar plane ticket to Italy, which finally got me out of that deep, dark hole.

The boyfriend was an avid traveler, and one January night, he found a sale for two hundred-dollar tickets to Milan for Valentine's Day. As soon as we bought the tickets, I said to myself, *"There's no way I'm going to Milan—one of the fashion capitals of the world—not feeling good about myself and not feeling cute for Valentine's Day."*

I became obsessed with finding new clothes. Partly because of my long work hours and partly because I didn't want to deal with fitting rooms, online shopping became my therapy. My increased weight now put me in a special fashion purgatory called "Size 14/16" where the largest sizes in Misses were too small and the smallest sizes in Plus were too big. I ordered clothes in all different shapes and silhouettes from all kinds of stores, trying to figure out what worked on this unfamiliar body.

As boxes of new clothes and shoes arrived at the apartment daily, the Minimalist Boyfriend constantly and grudgingly reminded me that traveling with multiple suitcases would be a major headache. With this new challenge to pack smart, I meticulously planned my travel wardrobe. Every item had to be comfortable, make me feel good, and have the ability to be worn multiple times during the rainy winter trip.

I finally decided on leather leggings, coated black jeans, a neon yellow cashmere sweater, a black off-the-shoulder sweater tunic, a striped T-shirt, a long grey cardigan, and chunky black combat boots. Each of these items fit me perfectly and even had a bit of edge I didn't know I would later need.

As I saw how good I could look, my confidence and love of clothes returned. I started replacing the NYC dresses in my closet with ones that worked for me now. Getting dressed each morning for work wasn't nearly as dreadful or dramatic.

Nothing makes a woman more beautiful than the belief that she is beautiful.

−SOPHIA LOREN

As we got closer to the trip, both of us experienced a palpable excitement. I was finally starting to feel like my old self again. When Valentine's Day arrived in Milan, I felt beautiful in my new favorite off-the-shoulder sweater, leather leggings, and chandelier earrings. It was a special night of pasta cooking classes and exploring the city. I rediscovered some of those lost parts of myself that night.

However, the magic didn't last. The last night in Italy, the boyfriend and I had an epic argument. According to him, everything wrong about our relationship had been because I "was no longer the woman he had met in NYC." I was devastated. Just as I was feeling better about myself, it wasn't enough for him. I pleaded with him to believe things would be different once we got home. Little did we both know how different.

After a few days of unspoken tension, we were driving home when I blurted out, "Are you going to be with me or not? Because I'm done being unhappy trying to please you." That ultimatum led to me moving out the next morning, combat boots and all.

After spending the next few weeks crying myself to sleep at my parents' house, my therapist helped me realize I had ended the relationship on my own terms and that was something to be proud of. That trip to Italy was a pivotal moment in increasing my confidence, all thanks to the new clothes that reminded me of my worthiness.

SUCCESS IS THE BEST REVENGE

That realization fueled me to rebuild my life and get "revenge" with success. I joined Weight Watchers and a flag football team. Partly because of my diligent meal prepping and partly because the office moved away from that Chick-fil-A, I was in the best shape of my life. I felt amazing and radiated confidence.

A few months into my transformation, my girlfriends and I took the obligatory "Sexy Singles" trip to Miami. Once again, I found inspiration in packing my suitcase. Instead of shopping online, I shopped my closet. The dresses from my old life in NYC fit even better than they had two years prior. I purchased new high heels and bikinis. I confidently (and drunkenly) strutted my stuff up and down Collins Avenue that weekend.

Upon returning to Atlanta, the job I hated got eliminated and I was placed on a new International Merchandising team with a boss I knew from my days at The Gap. Excited to be on a new team but also determined not to lose myself in my work again, I went looking for a "hobby."

I found image consulting. As I researched this novel concept of "getting paid to shop," I found an instructor back in NYC and spent a week there learning the fundamentals of style. I was hooked.

While I knew a lot about retail and the making of a garment, image consulting was about how to use those garments to enhance the wearer. By learning how to dress my own self through fit, color, and shape, I no longer felt like my body was something to be ashamed of. I wanted to share this gospel of freedom and started experimenting with friends. Word of mouth referrals led to paying clients, and I started a side hustle.

I spent a few months working with clients on the weekends or after work, but as my career took off, I put image consulting on hold. A year later, this business would become my saving grace.

While I was gaining notoriety at work for being a "dedicated team member" (i.e., overworked and underpaid), deep down, I was literally dying. The stress of long hours, travel, and conflicting leadership strategies created a literal weight in the middle of my chest. Determined to choose a better stress-coping mechanism than food, I found meditation.

Consuming all kinds of spiritual material and finding a church that felt like home led me to finding a peace and a sense of identity I had been searching for through new jobs and boyfriends. The Bible, podcasts, angel cards, crystal stones, and numerology were all part of my exploration. The time I spent each morning in silence, connecting to the spirit within, became my favorite part of the day. While I won't say I was walking on water, I definitely did "float" to work on a high each morning.

The more at peace I became with myself, the more all hell was breaking loose around me at work. My Zen bubble would burst each and every team meeting. It was becoming evident very quickly that I no longer could blend into that culture. In September 2016, after a few months of lots of prayer (and not that much planning), I made the leap of faith and quit my job. My plan was to "just shop for rich people" for a living. But God had bigger plans for me.

As I waited for the "rich housewives" to show up at my doorstep, I started working with women who were in unfulfilling jobs and relationships just as I had been. During our closet sessions, people shared stories of struggle, and I eventually quoted some of the books I had been reading. It began to dawn on me that my purpose was more than just shopping, but to help women find the lost parts of themselves, just as I found mine.

The years I spent struggling with accepting myself—no matter my size—helped me connect with other women. Because of these connections, I no longer feel like an outsider. I've found my tribe—incredibly talented, driven, and smart women who might be a little bit bruised by life but are still so beautiful.

> When you take care of yourself, you're a better person for others. When you feel good about yourself, you treat others better.
>
> —SOLANGE KNOWLES

I've also found my style. Now my wardrobe announces my presence instead of apologizing for it. Like most middle-aged women, I've become my mother. But thankfully, this has enabled me to relish the pretty details of a dress or the fabric of a well-made skirt. The Clothes Lover in me is proudly out of the closet, making each day "The Day" I wear my favorite pieces and show up fully as my best self. And while I still love a good pair of sweatpants, I now use them for lounging instead of hiding.

If you've made it through my entire life story, God bless you. I hope you see that I, too, have struggled with not only finding my style but finding myself. We'll explore this connection between soul and style throughout this book.

WORTHY WRAP-UP

1. Stop waiting for "The Day" for your life to magically change. Take one small action daily, even if it's just saying "no" to a chicken biscuit.
2. Discover a new hobby: something you're passionate about outside of work and family.
3. Develop your tribe: a community of friends who encourage you.
4. Find resources that further your personal and spiritual growth: church, therapy, support groups, classes, books.
5. Create a wardrobe that announces your presence instead of apologizes for it.

WORTHY WORDS

Today is the day I show up as my best self.

CHAPTER 2

GOLDEN

———

Looking back on my life and style evolution, I see that for my first thirty years, I was on the hunt for something. I jumped from city to city, job to job, boyfriend to boyfriend, hoping that, with each change, the puzzle pieces would magically come together and my life would make sense. Turns out the thing I was looking for was my Golden Buddha.

In his book, *Dare to Be Yourself*, Alan Cohen retells this famous and true story:

> Several hundred years ago in Thailand, there was a temple with a huge Golden Buddha. When word came to this village that an army was about to invade, the monks covered the Golden Buddha with mud and concrete so it looked like a stone Buddha and the invading army would perceive no value in it.
>
> Sure enough, the army rolled in and passed by the stone Buddha and had no reason to plunder it. Years passed, and after a time, the occupying army left the village. But by then, all of the monks who had covered

the Buddha had left the monastery or passed away. In fact, there remained no one left in the town who remembered that the Buddha's true nature was golden.

And then one day in 1957, a young monk was meditating at the base of the Buddha, and a little piece of mud chipped off, exposing its golden core. "Come quickly!" he shouted to the other monks. "The Buddha is golden!" Together they began to chip away the mud and mortar that had disguised the Buddha for so many years. Before long all of the facade had been removed, and the Golden Buddha was restored to its original splendor.[4]

Before I found my Golden Buddha, I was anxious and full of self-doubt. From the outside view, I had a charmed life— loving parents, stable household, amazing friends, and cool jobs in cool cities. The world should have been my oyster. But nothing made sense. Everything was a challenge. Life felt like a quantum physics exam that everyone but me had been given the answers to. The harder I pushed, the more I tried to guess my way through that test everyone else seemed to be acing. The question, *What is wrong with me?*" always loomed in my head.

This depressive cycle manifested itself in my wardrobe. My internal angst, loneliness, and confusion were thick layers of "mud and concrete," showing up as baggy sweatpants

---

4   Alan Cohen, *Dare to Be Yourself: How to Quit Being an Extra in Other Peoples Movies and Become the Star of Your Own* (New York: Ballentine Books, 1994), 3-4.

and mumu dresses. Not only was I trying to hide because I didn't fit in, but I was also trying to hide because I didn't want anyone to see my insecurity. I feared that if someone paid attention to me, they would see all that was wrong: the anxiety, the low self-esteem, the weight gain. I didn't even like myself, let alone know or care enough to dress myself. So I donned my invisible wardrobe.

I found temporary solace in all kinds of therapy; the kinds found on a couch, in a pill, and in a mall. But nothing could fill the gnawing and massive hole in my heart that needed to be filled by *something*. I just couldn't figure out what that something was.

One of the worst things about anxiety is that it makes you feel like you're the only person in the world feeling what you're feeling. In the depths of my despair, I felt so isolated, totally consumed with the idea that "everyone else" had it all figured out. But that's not at all the case. The American Psychiatric Association reports that approximately one in nine women will have a depressive episode this year.[5]

And while a depressive episode sounds clinical and scary, nearly all the women in my life have had one, or several, moments where life felt hard and heavy. When nothing they did felt good enough. When they didn't feel good enough.

It's hard to admit that those feelings of heaviness and nervousness are present, especially when we have the social

5   "Mental Health Disparities: Women's Mental Health," American Psychiatric Association, accessed on January 11, 2020.

status of degrees and titles. But it's okay to acknowledge those feelings. They suck and they hurt, but they're there and need to be worked through. I know now what I wish I knew then. These feelings are part of being human, and there's light at the end of the tunnel.

THERE'S NOTHING WRONG WITH US

Sometimes it takes a "dark night of the soul" to change how we choose to live. Thanks to a stressful job, I began to explore meditation and spirituality way beyond my occasional Sunday morning at whichever church was closest to whatever apartment I lived in at the time.

I found solace in the fact that there was more to me than the thoughts running through my head and started to consume literature on what that "more" was. As I read the spiritual works of Marianne Williamson, Michael Singer, Eckhart Tolle, and H. Emilie Cady, I came to see more of who I really was. These authors have become friends and family members in my head, whom I constantly reference.

From reading the works of "Aunt" Marianne, I learned about the transformative power of a loving God who transcends any religion; "Cool Uncle" Michael's work showed me how to surrender to the universe, even when it might not make logical sense; "Big Brother" Eckhart taught me how much power there is in the present moment; "Grandma" Emilie introduced me to the practice of affirming the truth and denying the lies. These books, and many more, helped me live with less chaos and more peace.

When I sat in silence meditating each morning, I got to know myself better. Instead of being consumed with shame, I changed the way I spoke to myself and started practicing self-compassion. I began to see the awesomeness of The Universe and myself. The layers of mud were finally chipping away.

> We talk to God—that is prayer; God talks
> to us—that is inspiration.
>
> —H. EMILIE CADY[6]

While uncovering my inner Golden Buddha is a lifelong journey, one of the biggest realizations I have had so far is that nothing was ever wrong with me. Nothing's wrong with you either. We were so unhappy because we didn't know who we are; we damn sure didn't know our worth.

GROUNDED

Five years of spiritual truth-seeking makes me *far* from an expert in answering life's greatest question of human existence. But I'm certain we are all perfect children of God and, therefore, are all inherently worthy. We deserve all the desires of our hearts, no matter how big. If it's hard for you to wrap your brain around that, trust me, I get it. Many of us have been told by other people, the media, and even our

---

6   H. Emilie Cady, *Lessons in Truth: A Course of Twelve Lessons in Practical Christianity* (Kansas City: Unity School of Christianity, 1919), 158.

own minds that so much is wrong with us that it's nearly impossible to know anything else.

One resource helpful in remembering who I truly am is *A Course in Miracles*. This big book is part New Age-bible and part daily devotional. Each lesson helps us see that the greatest, and most important, miracle of all is knowing the truth of our identities. The course determines that "your worth is established by God. As long as you dispute this, everything you do will be fearful...Nothing you do or think or wish or make is necessary to establish your worth." [7]

You don't need to do anything to earn your "keep" on Earth.

You're worthy of being here. In this moment, in this lifetime, you matter—not because of what you've accomplished; or the company you work for; or the degrees you have; or the relationship you're in; or what size you are. You matter because God created you, and you can't do (or not do) anything to change your worthiness. Any ideas to the contrary are layers of mud covering your Golden Buddha. These ideas are entirely false, driven out of not knowing or remembering who you truly are.

When we don't acknowledge our worthiness, we are caught up in a tornado of emotions and insecurities, getting tossed

---

7   Dr. Stephanie Schucman, *A Course in Miracles: Combined Volume* (Mill Valley: The Foundation for Inner Peace, 2007), 54.

around, trying to find validation everywhere outside of us. When we truly start to believe all of this, worthiness acts like gravity, grounding us in the sacred truths that we belong, we matter, and we have a purpose. As soon as we get anchored in our worthiness, everything in our life starts falling into place, including our wardrobes.

WORTHY WRAP-UP
1. The hunt for peace is an inside job. A new job, city, or relationship won't instantly solve everything.
2. Absolutely nothing is wrong with you—not a single, solitary thing.
3. You are a perfect child of God who is worthy of being here.

WORTHY WORDS
I am golden.

CHAPTER 3

FOUNDATION

———

New clothes are hard to wear when old beliefs are ruling your identity.

I've styled and shopped for hundreds of women. By the time my clients get to me, they realize the importance of their image and honoring all of who they are through their wardrobes. They just don't know *how* to do that and are willing to make the investment in my services and expertise.

But on rare occasions, when a client wasn't grounded in worthiness, not only was my work extremely difficult, it was also meaningless. She didn't like anything I selected for her. She responded to everything she put on with a frown or a refusal to look at herself in the mirror. Even when I finally convinced her that she looked great in a few things, I know she never wore them.

Without acknowledging your inner Golden Buddha, shopping is impossible. No matter what you put on, nothing is good enough to counter your muddy beliefs about yourself.

Until you know in the depths of your being that you matter, that you have a purpose in life, and that you're worthy of being seen in all your divine splendor, anything you wear will keep you invisible. Even if it's Dior, it will be mud.

To remove the mud and build a Worthy Wardrobe, we must first establish a foundation of who we really are. These "truths" will influence all the work we're about to do together on your wardrobe.

Some of these concepts might be a little (or a lot) of a stretch for you, or you may wonder what the hell they have to do with shopping. But as my story has proven, our outer image is merely a reflection of our inner thoughts and beliefs about ourselves. Once we truly know, accept, and love who we are on the inside, then we can enjoy how we look on the outside.

Here are my five universal Truths I hope you adopt as your own, along with an explanation of how they influence our worthiness.

#1 THE UNIVERSE IS MADE OUT OF AND GOVERNED BY SOURCE ENERGY

I'll borrow words from one of my favorite books, *You are a Badass*:

> Call it whatever you want- God, Goddess, The Big Guy, The Universe, Source Energy, Higher Power, The Grand Poobah, gut, intuition, Spirit, The Force, The Zone, The Lord, The Vortex, The Mother Lode-it doesn't matter...Whatever you choose to call it isn't important, what is important is that you start to develop an awareness of, and relationship with, the Source Energy...[8]

I'll even add a few more names to the mix: Father, Mother, The Man Upstairs, Infinite Intelligence, The Almighty. I choose to call this vast, all-encompassing, all-knowing, all-loving Presence "God." And because "God" doesn't get enough credit for also being feminine, I'll be referring to this energy as "She" for the rest of the book.

Activist Glennon Doyle puts to words how I also feel about pronoun-ing God: "I think it's ridiculous to think of God as anything that could possibly be gendered. But as long as the expression of God as female is unimaginable to many while the expression of God as male feels perfectly acceptable—and as long as women continue to be undervalued and abused

---

8   Jen Sincero, *You Are a Badass: How to Stop Doubting Your Greatness and Start Living an Awesome Life* (London: John Murray Learning, 2016), 30.

and controlled here on Earth—I'll keep [referring to God as "She."]"[9]

My practice of prayer, meditation, and journaling helps me to get to know God on an intimate level. In these moments, I am often in awe of the unconditional and unfathomable love this source has for me, and for you.

The experience of God, or in any case the possibility of experiencing God, is innate.

–ALICE WALKER

If sitting in stillness isn't quite your thing, then another great way to acknowledge and experience the awesomeness of God is to go outside. It can be your backyard or even the bench outside your office (that's where I used to go when I was three seconds away from snapping at my boss). Stand outside, look up, and appreciate the ecosystem. Take in the grandness and beauty of the world, even if it's just a cloud or a butterfly.

If you're feeling really stressed, take your shoes off and walk in the closest patch of grass you can find. As someone who isn't a fan of dirt or bugs, this idea used to gross me out, but now I appreciate the feeling of connection I gain by feeling my feet on the "solid ground" supporting us all.

---

9   Glennon Doyle, *Untamed* (New York: The Dial Press, 2020), 247.

#2 GOD CREATED A LAVISHLY ABUNDANT UNIVERSE

The solid ground supporting us is also the same Earth providing for our every need. God created a plentiful universe literally overflowing with progress and innovation. Despite what you may hear on the news, we live in a land of plenty. There's plenty of time, plenty of money, and plenty of possibility.

While I have the utmost respect for all religious texts, the Bible is the one I'm most familiar with, and maybe Paul the Apostle will convince you of the true nature of the universe. In his letter to the Corinthians, Paul writes, "God is able to bless you abundantly, so that in all things at all times, having all that you need, you will abound in every good work."[10]

When we can truly recognize how lavishly abundant the universe is, our fears of not having enough of anything subside. Is it always easy to live in this truth? Umm, no. I'm an entrepreneur and have been broker than broke far more times than I'd like to remember. However, my empty bank account had nothing to do with God, but it had everything to do with forgetting to choose faith over worry. The sooner I remembered that I live in a land of plenty, the sooner God opened the windows of heaven and poured out an overflowing blessing.

---

10   2 Corinthians 9:8 NIV

#3 GOD CREATED US AS DIVINE BEINGS

When it comes to our wardrobes, we often get consumed with our physical bodies—what we look like and how much we weigh. But we're not just our bodies. There's more to us than just our physical identity markers.

According to French philosopher Pierre Teilhard de Chardin, because God created us, we are spiritual beings on earth having a human experience. We are made up of three components: our physical bodies, our mental minds, and our spirits. As humans, one is not more important than the other. Each one contributes to helping us be our best selves. When one is neglected, our entire being is impacted. Only when we address all three can we best dress the body.

Let's briefly break down each:

- **The Body**: The physical body you're in. It's simple in theory but loaded with all kinds of baggage. What we like about ourselves, what we don't, how we're treated by others—so much of this is a direct result of our physical bodies. But those thoughts and feelings must be stored (and originated) somewhere.
- **The Mind**: The thing that thinks the thoughts that direct us each day. It's the logical part of us that functions during our waking hours. The "conscious mind" takes observations and experiences and applies judgment, determining if something is true, false, good, or bad. Those thoughts get stored and turn into actions, thanks to...
- **The Soul**, which is also called the "subconscious mind," is the deep center fed by the thoughts of your conscious

mind. Your soul is connected to the extraordinary capacity of infinite power and intelligence that governs the universe. Pretty cool, right? But here's the kicker; your subconscious mind is 100 percent reliant on the conscious mind, which is why it's called the "subjective mind." It's "subject" to the influence of the conscious mind.

Every day, we're bombarded with messages of not being skinny enough, curvy enough, wealthy enough, or good enough. It's the conscious mind's job to filter the messages, determining which is true and what will become a belief in our subconscious minds.

> It is confidence in our bodies, minds, and spirits that allows us to keep looking for new adventures.
>
> —OPRAH WINFREY

These "truths" influence what we think and feel about ourselves, which impact how we treat and dress ourselves. When we look at our bodies in the mirror, our conscious minds see a bulge and think, *Ugh, I gained five pounds.* That loaded thought is heard by the subconscious mind, which can turn it into, *I'm fat and ugly and unlikeable.* The next time we go shopping, if we even go, we bring those beliefs with us into the dressing room.

Shopping becomes impossible because no matter what we put on, nothing is good enough to counter our beliefs about ourselves. So we don an Invisible Wardrobe just good enough to get us through our day. But this isn't how we're meant to live.

#4 AS DIVINE BEINGS, WE'RE INHERENTLY PERFECT

The more life we've lived, the more negative messages we've heard and tough moments we've survived. This resiliency has gotten us through a lot, but it can also cause the filter in the conscious mind to malfunction. We become extremely hard on ourselves, finding fault everywhere, forgetting that we're Divine Beings, and ignoring everything amazing about us.

Well, let this be your reminder that because God created each one of us and because God is "all-knowing," no mistakes are made. Therefore, as children of God, we are each an expression of Her and are, therefore, inherently perfect. "Aunt" Marianne Williamson writes in her first book, *A Return to Love*, which, by the way, was Oprah-approved (#goals), "You are a child of God. You were created in a blinding flash of creativity, a primal thought when God extended Himself in love...The perfect you isn't something you need to create, because God already created it."[11]

When I'm hard on myself and feeling like I'm not as good as someone else on social media, it's because, in that moment, I've forgotten that I'm perfect. I don't mean in the arrogant way of thinking like, *"I'm better than anyone else."* My

---

11   Marianne Williamson, *A Return to Love: Reflections on the Principles of a Course in Miracles* (San Francisco: HarperOne, 2009), 29.

feelings of doubt and comparison are an indication that my conscious mind has forgotten that I'm a child of God and am, therefore, no less special and no more special than anyone else.

To prevent those negative thoughts from sticking to my soul, I affirm to myself: *"I am perfect just as I am."* I repeat it over and over, sometimes silently, sometimes aloud (depending on where I am). The more I tell myself, the more I believe it.

Give it a try right now. Tell yourself you're perfect. Because you are. And based on the laws of the universe, it's impossible that you are anything but.

My inherent perfection doesn't mean I can't benefit from a flattering dress or little concealer, blush, and hair color. Choosing to adorn myself with makeup and different hairstyles doesn't mean I'm not perfect as I am. It just means this is the way I choose to present my perfection to the world. Whether it's a fully done face or wigs that change based on your mood, as long you're confident, then your expression is perfect.

"Big Brother" Eckhart Tolle adds, "You are the universe, expressing itself as Human for a little while." It's amazing to think we are all pieces of the bigger Universe. God chose me and you as the ways She wanted to come down to Earth. We really must be something, and we certainly must have a reason for being here.

#5 EACH OF US HAS A PURPOSE

One of my favorite scriptures is: "'For I know the plans I have for you,' declares the Lord, 'plans to prosper you and not to harm you, plans to give you hope and a future.'"[12]

As cliché as it sounds, all of us are here for a reason. I believe that reason is to be of service to others as the expression of God's love. The way we complete our assignments of service is unique to each of us. While our jobs pay the bills, our purpose is how we contribute to the greater good of the world. Some serve others as teachers, bankers, or lawyers. Others serve as mothers, bishops, or writers. Whatever you're called to do and wherever you are right now is exactly where you're supposed to be to show love and serve.

Even if you hate your job (I've been there), you're in that cubicle on a divine assignment to do good in some way. The sooner you figure out what that purpose is, the more enjoyable your work will become. Even if it's a stretch, look for the ways your presence impacts your team and the end customer. Take pride in those contributions and assess how you can parlay them into what you ultimately desire to do.

In the meantime, whatever your purpose is right now, its fulfillment depends on being confident in who you are—spirit, mind, and body. That means knowing you're the perfect person for the job at hand and dressing like it. When we honor ourselves with a stylish wardrobe appropriate for our unique divine assignments, we give gravitas to our missions.

---

12   Jeremiah 29:11 (NIV)

We command respect and garner attention to our work for the right reasons.

I truly believe God doesn't want you looking miserable or "covered in mud" while you're out doing Her work. After all, what kind of spokesperson of love would you be if you look like you don't love yourself?

We are all God's children, and it's time we start looking the part.

Maybe this is just me, but I find it mind-blowing that we are perfect divine beings inhabiting a plentiful universe on a divine assignment of purpose. How amazing is it to know that this inherent divinity makes us worthy of our heart's desires?

WORKING ON WORTHINESS

Knowing your worth doesn't happen overnight. It takes a conscious decision to choose a new way of thinking about yourself. Dr. Barbara Lewis King, bishop and founder of my beloved church, Hillside International Truth Center, is also my spiritual grandmother, as we have bonded over our love of fine wine and fine clothes.

Inspired by one of her sermons, here are some exercises to strengthen your spiritual muscles.

LOVE YOURSELF.

"Self-love" is such a vague term thrown around everywhere that it can be hard to know how to actually start the practice of loving yourself. Well, it starts with looking at the woman in the mirror. Literally. Each morning, stand in front of the mirror. And before you criticize the bags under your eyes or the pimples on your chin, look yourself straight in the eyes and say aloud, *"I love you."* Say it over and over and over. It will feel weird at first, but I guarantee you will feel different after a few minutes and a few days of this practice.

I have also used this practice in my "Body Love" workshops. Attendees stand in front of a full-body mirror and say, *"I love you and I forgive you"* to any specific body part they might not be thrilled about. The more we can love all of ourselves, the easier everything else becomes.

> You, yourself, as much as anybody in the entire universe, deserve your love and affection.
>
> —BUDDHA

GUARD YOUR THOUGHTS.

The subconscious mind is extremely powerful but extremely sensitive. Don't let anything into your mind that doesn't inspire or uplift you. That might mean tuning out the news, certain kind of music, or even your nagging mother. It might mean tuning out yourself. Start watching what you say about yourself and to yourself.

If you wouldn't say it to your best friend or a newborn baby, don't say it to yourself.

STAY IN CONSTANT COMMUNION.
While morning meditation and prayer time is critical to starting your day with the right intentions, God wants to hear from you throughout the day. As you're making your coffee or driving to the office, have an ongoing conversation with God. Tell Her what you're struggling with. Ask Her to show you the next best step. Thank Her for both your small and big blessings.

The more you talk with God, the better you'll get at listening to Her as well. That "still, small voice" within you will begin to speak louder and you'll be more secure in your connection to the Source.

Without a firm foundation of Truth about your divinity and worthiness, it's impossible to have style.

Getting dressed becomes an enjoyable experience once you know that no matter what the reflection in the mirror is showing, you have an inner golden divine essence that deserves to be expressed.

So now let's get to work on adorning the heavenly being that you are with a Worthy Wardrobe.

WORTHY WRAP-UP
1. God created us and the lavishly abundant universe we live in.
2. You are a perfect, divine being with a body, mind, and spirit.
3. You're here for a reason. Discover how you want to fulfill your divine assignment and look good while doing it.
4. Practice stillness. Give your soul a chance to connect with God. Prayer, mediation, journaling, and being outdoors are all great ways to get closer to Her.
5. Think and speak loving thoughts about yourself and your body.

WORTHY WORDS
I am divine.

CHAPTER 4

FAIRY GODMOTHER

I am writing this chapter on January 1, 2020, the day when people everywhere are starting diets and exercise regimes. So many of us have spent the entire previous year, or decade, in a constant battle with our bodies. As women, we've all been given the subconscious message that something (or many things) is wrong with our bodies and certain areas need to be hidden or "fixed." On January 1, many of us start that new fad diet, go to the gym to firm up this, shimmy into a girdle to smooth out or push up that—all in an attempt to feel better about how we look.

> With the new day comes new strength and new thoughts.
>
> −ELEANOR ROOSEVELT

According to *U.S. News & World Report*, the failure rate for New Year's resolutions is about 80 percent, with most people losing their resolve by mid-February.[13] This means for the remaining eleven months, we're back to the negative self-talk about how we look, often avoiding shopping and mirrors altogether. Or, in my case, succumbing to those mumus of loose maxi dresses and ex-boyfriend's sweaters.

When I first started styling women, I was shocked to discover my clients had the same negative thoughts about their bodies that I've struggled with. I would walk into the closets of these beautiful women with amazing bodies, thinking our closet sessions would be easy breezy. But no less than ten minutes in, the comments of "my boobs are too small" or my "stomach is so big" would come, sounding just like I used to. I started to see that I wasn't the only woman who had identified herself with a false narrative about her body.

DITCH THE PITY PARTY

Not liking how we look often feels like a badge of honor women bond over. In a scene from the cult classic movie *Mean Girls,* the popular girl gang all looks at themselves in the mirror and tries to one-up each other on what they dislike about their bodies: "My hips are HUGE," complains Karen. "I hate my calves," whines Gretchen. "At least you guys can wear halters. I've got man shoulders," declares Regina. The complaining continues when the crew turns to Cady, expecting her to join in on the pity party. "Ummm, I hate my breath in the morning," says the newbie.

---

13   Marla Tabaka, "Most People Fail to Achieve Their New Year's Resolution. For Success, Choose a Word of the Year Instead," *Inc.,* January 7, 2019.

As silly as this scene sounds, there's an unspoken rule that disliking something about your body makes you relatable and likable. Downplaying your looks somehow makes other women feel more comfortable. No one does this more than one of my friends, Stephanie.

Stephanie and I became close during college. At twenty-two, Stephanie wore a size two on her long and lean 5'7" frame, with the best set of boobs I've ever seen—natural or enhanced. Being teased as a kid for being a "string bean," Stephanie griped about lacking the hips and butt I resented having my entire life. Meanwhile, I was so jealous of the cheap but cute club outfits she could easily purchase from the Junior's department.

You have been criticizing yourself for years and it hasn't worked. Try approving of yourself and see what happens.

— LOUISE HAY

Around the age of twenty-eight, Stephanie sprouted a butt seemingly overnight. Suddenly, her long legs were now enhanced by a curvaceous bum. She looked amazing. But instead of being excited that her wish for hips was answered, Stephanie constantly complained that none of her signature jumpsuits fit.

We would go shopping together to find new clothes for her new shape and, honestly, it was exhausting. She held a never-ending soliloquy of what was now wrong with her body. Most times she left stores empty-handed, refusing to buy anything larger than the size two she was accustomed to buying. Size was a mental minefield for her, and with each shopping trip, an explosion of frustration and negative self-talk was sure to detonate.

A FIGMENT OF IMAGINATION

While Stephanie's resistance to size was a bit extreme, the battlefield she had created around size wasn't entirely her own creation. In a Facebook video created by Attn, an issues-driven media organization that produces videos and articles aimed at telling the truth behind lots of common practices, plus-sized supermodel Ashley Graham uncovers the loaded history behind the crazy concept of sizing:

> Historically, women had their clothes tailor-made. If you had the money, someone could do this for you, and if not, you could sew them yourself. But around the Second World War, ready-to-wear clothing grew in popularity. In the 1940s, the government commissioned a major study in hopes of creating a size standard for women.

> Unfortunately, the findings only included data from a very small group of white women. So it wasn't very helpful. Ten years later, a standard sizing system

finally got approved and looked at height, bust size, and girth. But the government dropped it in 1983.

So today it's like the Wild West when it comes to sizing. You will have completely divergent fits across all retailers. A size six pair of jeans can vary by up to five inches at the waistband. One study found that a size of four had an even larger discrepancy at 8.5 inches.[14]

I know firsthand the madness of sizing; as part of the merchandising teams at The Gap, Old Navy, and Banana Republic, I was a part of creating it. Don't hate me, I'm attempting to right my wrongs by telling you what the retail industry doesn't want you to know: the concept of "size" is a figment of the imagination—the imagination of the decision-makers of each clothing brand to be exact.

"Wait, what?" You ask. "How can size be imaginary? Isn't it just a simple concept of measurements?" Hardly.

Size has to do with identity—not your identity, but the identities of the brand and the brand's desired customer. To be successful, any brand—whether it's clothing or laundry detergent—must determine their target customer, the person who will consistently buy their products. To get that person to become an actual customer, retailers have to get in the customer's head, observing minute details about their lifestyle: their age, their income level, where they live, their marital status, if they have any kids, and the other places they like to shop. After doing all this research, each brand

---

14 *Attn,* "One Size Fits None," December 26, 2019, video, 4:06.

creates an avatar, a mythical person for whom every single decision is made—including size.

During my tenure at Old Navy, it was my job as a merchant to know everything about our hypothetical and imaginary customer, "Jenny," a middle-classed, Midwestern thirty-one-year-old married mom, to ensure our product decisions were to her liking. Based on Jenny, we found a fit model whose body matched how we imagined Jenny's body would look after 2.5 kids. We considered the size of her bust, waist, hips, arms, and her height. We designated that fit model to be our "standard size six" and scaled our measurements up a certain percent to be a size eight and down a certain percent to be a size four.

Down the hall at our sister brand, Banana Republic, their fit model looked different than ours. Their target customer lived a totally different life than our Jenny. Despite both brands being owned by the same parent company, a size six pair of jeans at Old Navy fit totally different than a size six pair at Banana Republic. And as leadership and brand strategies changed over the years, so did the specifications for the standard size six.

According to *Wall Street Journal* reporter Suzanne Kapner,[15] what we as consumers call "crazy," the retail industry calls "competitive advantage." So don't expect consistency across brands any time soon. The next time you go into your favorite store to stock up on your favorite pants and they don't

---

15 Suzanne Kapner, "It's Not You. Clothing Sizes Are Broken," *The Wall Street Journal,* December 16, 2019.

quite fit the same, don't beat yourself up and regret having French fries last night, and please don't be like Stephanie and refuse to try on the next size up.

Instead, realize that a corporate office somewhere made a business decision, causing a change in identity of the *one* woman for whom these pants were custom made. If you really think about this concept of a mythical muse of a customer and a fit model on the other side of the world that you'll probably never meet, it's crazy to expect garments from any store to fit you perfectly right off the rack. In fact, it's practically impossible.

No one knows what the size tag says on your clothes, they just know when something doesn't fit. So give yourself and your body a break and buy the size that fits you best, no matter what it is.

After giving birth to her first child, my friend, Stephanie, is currently wearing a size fourteen and is even more self-conscious about her baby weight. One day while shopping together, she confided that when she looks back on old pictures, she's amazed that she ever complained about her body. "It's crazy that I was so hard on myself when I was wearing a size two," she recalls. "It's time I finally start to appreciate this body."

If chicken soup is the cure for a common cold, finding what works on her new body has helped Stephanie with the negative self-talk. On a recent shopping trip, she avoided landmines thanks to this new awareness. By being willing to try new things and accept her current size, Stephanie left the mall with several empire dresses that show off her statuesque legs while concealing her tummy. She felt excited to wear these dresses for her big meeting days. Off the shoulder and deep V necklines on flowy tops showed off her "impossibly perky, even after a baby" rack, and her straight-fit boyfriend jeans created an elongating silhouette that is slimming overall.

> Even though it will never be flat again, my stomach's still my favorite because it reminds me of my greatest achievement: my babies.
>
> —ISLA FISHER

We actually had fun on this shopping trip. Thanks to having a closet of options that honor who she is now, Stephanie's confidence is steadily increasing—so much so that she even shared a picture of herself in a swimsuit on social media, resulting in applauds and encouragement from so many women. Her decision to not self-abandon and actually do the work it takes to style her body is paying off.

SIZE VERSUS SHAPE

If you're like Stephanie and have been held hostage by your size, I'd like to liberate you a little bit by introducing the concept of shape—as in the shape of your body. Think of your size as an approximate indicator of your weight and stature. Your body shape is determined by where you hold most of that weight and stature. Thousands of books and websites are dedicated to helping you determine what your body shape is, so I won't go into detail here. But it's important to distinguish between size and shape for a few reasons.

We inherently prefer symmetry and balance. Our eye finds proportionally symmetrically things more "beautiful" than off-balance things. That is why an hourglass figure, featuring a full top half and equally full bottom with a small waist is the most idealized shape in art and fashion. However, few women actually have this shape. Most of us are born with one area larger than the other. Clothes are our secret weapon in creating an optical illusion of the desired hourglass.

For example, my shape is smaller on top, bigger on the bottom (commonly referred to as a "pear"). To "fake an hourglass," I wear tops that feature bright colors, patterns, and more voluminous details to create balance to my heftier hips. This trick also draws attention to my smaller upper half while downplaying hips that don't need any more attention.

Women with broader shoulders, do the exact opposite. They have a "party with their pants" and keep their tops simple. Knowing what area of your body you want to draw attention to and what area you want to camouflage helps your overall shape look amazing.

Getting intimate with your body shape is also beneficial because it gives you more flexibility when it comes to size. As a pear shape, I know I need more room on my bottom half. When shopping for dresses, I know that an A-line shape will allow me to go down to as small as a size eight, because the silhouette is accommodating at the bottom. But when it comes to a straight cut shift dress, I know I'll need to try on at least a size twelve. The straighter the cut is, the less forgiving in the hips. By the time said shift dress fits across my derriere, it's way too big in my chest. Definitely a bummer, but not at all a reason to leave it if I love everything else about the dress.

YOUR FAIRY GODMOTHER

Instead of putting so much pressure on yourself and your favorite store to find pants or dresses that fit your exact body shape perfectly, lower your expectations and find yourself a damn good tailor.

"A who?" you ask. A tailor, someone whose sole purpose is to make clothes fit and flatter you perfectly. Think of them as the Fairy Godmothers and Godfathers of clothing, taking a thrift store dress that makes you look like a pumpkin and turning you into the belle of the ball, or the interview. For the few of you who have a tailor, you might only use them for special occasion pieces or to maybe get your pants hemmed. You're selling yourself and your tailor short. Because so few clothes fit anyone perfectly, a tailor should be used for anything that you want to feel like a million bucks in—which should be every single thing, except maybe sweatpants.

I am genuinely dismayed when I meet grown women who don't patronize a tailor and instead choose to struggle with finding clothes that fit. By having an expert who can adjust clothes to make them work for you, you're free to go into a store knowing whatever you find will probably need some adjustments, and anything that does fit perfectly is an awesome surprise bonus.

Kiya Tomlin is a tailoring expert and owner of her own custom clothing line. In an article for website Refinery 29, she explains why tailoring for women isn't as common as it used to be:

> When mass-produced clothes first emerged, they were not created as a complete replacement for custom-made clothing, but more of an economical and convenient shortcut. People at that time understood ready-to-wear clothing was not supposed to fit you right off the rack, and there would still be a need to tailor these pieces.
>
> As styles became looser in the '60s and '70s, less tailoring was required, and eventually fewer people learned to sew. We came to think of tailoring anything beyond a hem as unusual. For the last few decades, we have been trying to make our bodies fit the clothes when,

in reality, we should be making the clothes fit our bodies."[16]

Hear that? Instead of shaming, Spanx-ing, or starving our bodies to fit clothes that were never meant to fit us, we all should be allowing our Fairy Godmothers to work their magic and make the clothes fit us.

YOU'RE PERFECT BECAUSE GOD MADE YOU

One of my real-life Fairy Godmothers is my aunt, Thomasena Reynolds, or as I affectionately call her, "Aunt Sine." Aunt Sine just recently closed her tailoring shop after an impressive forty-eight years in business. She's fitted congressmen, ladies who lunch, and all of the who's who in Columbia, South Carolina.

When I interviewed her for this book, this was the first piece of advice she gave me:

> The main thing is a woman should be happy with who she is. If a woman complains about her size, I tell her, "Look, God made you and you need to be happy. You're perfect because God made you. You need to accept your size and love it for what it is. Clothes only enhance what you are."

---

16   Aemilia Madden, "A Real Girl's Guide to Tailoring: What's Worth It (and What to Skip)," *Who What Wear,* October 25, 2018.

Fairy Godmother, indeed. While not all tailors will reference God when they're fitting you, a good tailor should be able to do the following fixes:

#1 SHORTEN ANYTHING THAT NEEDS SHORTENING

This is an obvious one for most of us, as many women get their pants or skirts hemmed. But shortening also applies to your upper half. I've sent several petite clients to my tailor to get not only the sleeves of their shirts shortened but also the length. If you're on the petite side (about 5'4" and under), tops that fall past your waist can look like a nightgown on you.

The longer the top, the shorter your legs look; the shorter your legs look, the shorter you look; the shorter you look, the less lean you look. Taking a few inches off the bottom can work wonders.

#2 LENGTHEN ANYTHING THAT NEEDS LENGTHENING

At 5'10", I get lots of my pants taken out at the hem. However, lengthening is a trick that most women don't use to their advantage. Remember, the longer something is, the leaner you'll look. The best place this applies is with dresses and skirts.

While there's some bit of variation, according to Aunt Sine, the most flattering hem length is at the middle or just past your knee. "For example, you, Morgan, have big hips." Yes, thanks Aunt Sine. "If you wear a dress that's too short, you'll look wider and thicker," she lovingly advises. No, thank you.

Since a lot of clothes don't leave extra length in the hem, one way to avoid the stumpy effect is to order skirts in Tall, even if you're not. This will give you a few inches to play with to get the perfect length for you.

#3 TAKE IN ANYTHING THAT'S TOO BIG

Because I'm pear-shaped, any one piece (dresses or jumpsuits) is a challenge for me. If it fits these hips, it's way too big at my chest. My tailor is a card-carrying member of my personal itty-bitty-titty community, getting up close and personal with my boobs to determine how much excess fabric needs to get cut for my perfect fit.

If, instead, you're blessed with a bountiful chest and button-up shirts are a challenge, buy the biggest size that eliminates the risk of you popping someone's eye out with a button. Then have your Fairy Godmother create princess seams in the back, thereby tastefully showing off your curves and eliminating the pumpkin look.

When in doubt, always go up a size (or two). A tailor can work miracles with extra fabric, but if it's already too tight, you might be out of luck.

#4 SNATCH A WAIST

You know that extra fabric sitting around your waist when your jeans fit the hips but are too big up top? The answer to that gap is not a belt. It's a tailor. By creating a fitted waistline in your jeans or slacks, you eliminate the risk of the dreaded "whale tail." (Google "whale tail waistline" to see exposed backside and thong from poorly fitting pants.)

A fitted waistline also helps you create the illusion of a curvy, lean hourglass. For the short-legged, taking up the waist in a dress can also do wonders for your shape. This literally means cutting the dress into two parts and bringing the bottom half up to your natural waist so your legs look longer. Again, longer legs, leaner look.

#5 SNAP OR ZIP IT UP

I once found a beautiful forest green Sherpa-lined hooded anorak coat on the clearance rack. The hood and knee length made it perfect for my upcoming February trip to New York City. The problem was that when I zipped it up, it was too tight for me to walk in.

Since walking and a zipped-up coat are both necessities for NYC, something had to be done. And leaving this sixty-dollar coat for someone else was not an option. To the fabric store I went, new coat in hand, asking to be shown some double zippers.

These are the zippers that, once zipped, can be opened up at the bottom. I took said zipper to my Fairy Godmother, and for thirty-five dollars, my new coat and zipper allowed me to keep my chest covered while also giving my hips some walking room. This ninety-five-dollar anorak is now my winter staple.

In addition to zippers, I've seen tailors add secret snaps to keep a blouse closed or hide bra straps on a sleeveless dress. While this may sound a bit "frivolous," these little tweaks prevent you from having to "discreetly" add a safety pin (don't you dare!).

> ## Be yourself. Know your proportions. And have a good tailor.
>
> – RUPAUL

Did that trip to the fabric store and then the tailor and then back to tailor to pick up the jacket sound like a whole lot of extra time and work to you? I'll be the first to admit that taking items to a tailor is an extra step in the process of dressing yourself. Unfortunately, most Fairy Godmother tailors don't magically show up in our closets when we cry over not having anything to wear. While some do make house calls, most of us have to make time to make the magic happen.

MAKE THE INVESTMENT

In addition to time, tailoring also requires a financial investment. If you're in a major city, a good tailor isn't cheap, but they will be worth every single penny. Instead of only altering your "fancy" clothes, I *highly* suggest (okay, maybe even demand) that you also alter your bargain finds, assuming you'll get lots of wear out of them. A $19.99 dress from an off-price store that has been altered for thirty-five dollars will look exponentially more expensive than a too-tight two-hundred-dollar dress from a department store.

I remember one day going to my salon after a big meeting with a corporate executive and my aesthetician raving about my orange shift dress, the minute I walked in. "OH MY GOD! In all these years, I've never seen you look so good," squealed Shanna. "That dress looks like it was *made for you.*"

Well, it kind of was. I had found this orange tweed sleeveless dress online for less than sixty bucks. I ordered the twelve Tall, and, of course, when it came in, my bra was showing in the gaps under my arms. Good Ole Fairy Godmother snatched those armholes right up for maybe forty dollars (a heavy fabric like tweed can sometimes cost a little more to alter), and I sashayed around town looking like a million bucks.

Bad news: looking good in your clothes takes a bit of effort. Good news: The more you work at it, the easier it becomes. Amazing news: You're absolutely worth it.

Remember what Aunt Sine said: "You're perfect because God made you."

WORTHY WRAP-UP

Here are some new resolutions when it comes to your body (even if it's not January 1 anymore):

1. Stop complaining about your body—aloud or in your head. It doesn't benefit you or anyone else within earshot.
2. Don't let size sorcery win. Be willing to try on a variety of brands and sizes to find what works for your body.
3. Find a Fairy Godmother, a.k.a. a tailor. Visit her frequently for everyday and special occasion items.

WORTHY WORDS

I am perfect because God made me.

CHAPTER 5

BODY LOVE

———

To go to a tailor, you first must have clothes that need to be altered, which is where the biggest struggle lies for many curvy women. Size sorcery aside, shopping can be far from a "godly" experience. Sixty-eight percent of American women wear a size fourteen or above, including me.[17]

However, most mainstream brands only carry up to a size twelve in store. Yup, that's quite the cruel conundrum, even for Ashley Graham, who laments that while she may be one of the world's most sought-after models, "If I left set right now and headed to the mall, it's possible I wouldn't find anything in my size." Per my own experience of walking out of that 5-7-9 store empty-handed, I'm all too familiar with this frustrating experience.

To avoid disappointment, lots of us get stuck waiting for "The Day." That's "The Day" we'll finally love everything about our bodies and go shopping for clothes we love. *That's* when we'll "finally be happy," we say. We forebode joy to a mythical destination of perky boobs, flat tummies, slim hips, and amazing

———

17   *Attn,* "One Size Fits None."

legs. But for most of us, that day doesn't come. For some, the roadblock to body love is leftover pregnancy weight. For other women, the roadblocks are the battle scars from illness.

In word, deed, and wardrobe, my friend Montrice has always been a perfectionist. In the three years I've known her, she has never misspoken a word or had a hair out of place. Montrice confided in me that ten years ago, her world was turned upside down with a diagnosis of Crohn's disease. She shared her years-long journey of suffering from a surgery to remove parts of her intestines, resulting in her having to permanently use an ostomy pouch. I was in total shock when she told me this.

Montrice explained, "For so long, I did everything I could to hide my bag from everyone. Every outfit had to be loose enough and long enough to hide it because I didn't want anyone to think of me as 'disabled.' I don't want sympathy, but I knew I had to share with you one particular story that helped me look at my situation differently."

While driving to a job interview, Montrice's ostomy pouch leaked, spilling all over her favorite magenta blouse. "After shedding a few tears out of frustration," she recalls, "I calmly called the hiring manager and told her I was in an accident and would be a few minutes late. I rushed home, changed my clothes, and made it to the interview. When the woman I was meeting with inquired about the accident, I came clean and told her the truth. Her response blew me away: 'Oh my goodness, I was just diagnosed with Crohn's. Can you please share with me your experience?'"

Montrice's struggle was now the saving grace for another woman and she no longer is afraid to share the truth about her body. Whether it's wearing skinny jeans or a bikini to the beach, Montrice wears her clothes and her pouch with pride, as she knows, no matter what the condition, her body is perfect just the way it is.

At the end of the day, we can endure much more than we think we can.

— FRIDA KAHLO

When I was in high school, I did an independent study on art created by women diagnosed with breast cancer. The poems, photographs, and illustrations about grieving and accepting the loss of a breast hit my seventeen-year-old self hard. In my art notebook, I wrote, "Wow, these images really put things in perspective for me. I mean, here I am bitching about how I hate my breasts and some women are losing their breasts to stay alive. Ain't that something."

We women are so hard on ourselves. The impossible standards of beauty imposed upon us prevent us from appreciating and loving our bodies for doing what it's meant to do—keep us alive.

Instead of hiding or fighting or shaming our bodies, let's focus on honoring them no matter their state or size.

DOING THE WORK

It takes a conscious decision to be willing to do the work of dressing a body you haven't always been proud of. Recent PhD recipient Samantha shared with me her story of coming to peace with her body. During the five stressful years of putting academics before everything else, Samantha gained fifty pounds and was relying on sweatpants and long duster cardigans for class every day.

She was forced to deal with the challenges of her new body only during special occasions or nights out. That's when she realized just how little of her wardrobe she could physically wear. "I couldn't wear my jeans because they were so tight and were an uncomfortable reminder of my weight gain," shared Samantha, "So I would try to dress up my leggings as much as possible. But if my attendance wasn't required, I often wouldn't go because I didn't have anything to wear."

Just as my trip to Italy forced me to upgrade my wardrobe, a move to a new city prompted Samantha to finally start honoring her current body with new clothes. "Now that I've graduated," Samantha said, "this move feels like a fresh start for my career and my wardrobe. I've told myself to forget about the mediums I used to wear and buy the XL, or even the XXL, if I need to. Even though shopping has been more of a challenge, it feels great to have real pants in my closet that actually fit me. I wear my sweatpants a lot less now, and actually make the effort to get dressed, even if I'm just running errands."

Thankfully, mainstream stores are extending their size ranges and plus-sized specific brands are becoming much more prevalent, making it easier to shop for flattering and stylish clothes that fit a larger-sized body. There's now no excuse not to make the effort and seek out clothes that fit your current body shape and size.

> To me, beauty is about being comfortable in your own skin. It's about knowing and accepting who you are.
>
> —ELLEN DEGENERES

Jessica was wearing a size thirty-two when we worked together, and instead of hiding behind big, black, and baggy items, she was ready to show up as her best self. Was it a challenge at times? Absolutely. Did she or I give up? Hell no. Instead of going to the mall, I went to her home with several online shopping carts filled with suggestions. We sat down and talked through every option, making decisions based on what she already owned and her lifestyle needs.

Once the items arrived, I returned to unpack and assess what stayed, what got returned, and what needed to be touched by a Fairy Godmother. Bright red pants that were too long were hemmed to just above the ankle—one of the most slimming parts on any woman's body. We lengthened beautifully printed dresses to just below the knee to create more coverage; fixed necklines that showed too much cleavage by taking up the shoulders; shortened sleeves of blazers and blouses to stop at the forearm, the narrowest part of the arm; and adjusted zippers and buttons to give more room.

Thanks to these alterations, Jessica radiated confidence in every room she entered.

Do not let your weight stop you from feeling good about your image. No one sees the size on the tag, but everyone sees if you've made an effort.

> *Instead of excusing your wardrobe because of your size, show the world that you're worthy of being seen.*

You have my total permission to put this book down right now, get online, and find your new favorite dress, pants, or sexy blouse—whatever will help you feel as beautiful as you are. And if it arrives and it's not the perfect fit, don't dismay. Order another size or find yourself a Fairy Godmother.

FINE WINE

Once that new blouse arrives, you might realize that a certain pair of assets aren't sitting in the right place. Putting new clothes on top of old bras reminds me of one of Jesus' parables: "No man putteth new wine into old bottles; else the new wine will burst the bottles, and be spilled, and the bottles shall perish. But new wine must be put into new bottles; and both are preserved."[18]

While boobs don't usually get better with age (unless you've had some work done—if so, more power to you!), they are like wine in that they need good and sturdy containers. Otherwise, they spill out everywhere, causing lumps and bumps and killing any chance of a flattering outfit.

Our bras are the first thing we put on in the morning. They're constantly with us, supporting two of our most feminine parts and covering up our sacred heart chakra. I've seen lots of women in their skivvies, and I can tell a whole lot about what a woman thinks of herself by the condition of her bras.

When I see a frayed and worn bra without any structure, it tells me this woman doesn't believe she's worthy of being supported. She hasn't created the time or allocated the funds to put herself first in this significant part of her wardrobe. If you look down at your chest right now and see gaps in the middle, or spillage on the sides, or your shoulders have indentations from your straps, Jesus is literally weeping for you right now. Do better.

Life is like underwear; change is good.

–UNKNOWN

---

18   Luke 5:37 (NIV).

Most expert fitters suggest that because our boobs change with age, weight fluctuations, and even birth control, it's important to get fitted at least once a year. Once a *year*, not once a decade like many women I've worked with—if they've ever been professionally fitted at all. And by fitting, I mean going to a store that doesn't cater to teenagers or supermodels. High-end department stores usually do a great job training their staff, but also search to see if a small boutique in your city can give you excellent customer service and offer a wide variety of sizes and price points.

Earlier this year, I took my good friend Noelle to my favorite Atlanta-area lingerie boutique. This shopping trip happened after she confided in me that she had never been fitted for a bra. Never. In her entire life. Here's how Noelle justified her lack of bra knowledge: "My mom has big boobs too, so I just assumed I wore a similar size of 38DD."

Because Noelle was always wearing loose cut tops, I wasn't 100 percent sure she was wrong about her size, but I definitely had my doubts. "Let's just go to my favorite bra store and see if you're right," I cajoled. "We'll make a day trip out of it and grab lunch after."

By the time we got to lunch, Noelle needed several drinks to quiet her shock. "THIRTY-TWO GEEEE!" She kept exclaiming when we left the store. "I can't believe I'm a 'G'! That's crazy to me."

"Umm, have you looked at your boobs, Noelle?" I sarcastically countered. "It's actually not that crazy."

Noelle had made the common mistake of equating big boobs to a high underband number. She had been wearing a band four sizes too big, and a cup three sizes too small. Her cup had runneth over.

Now that her boobies are preserved in beautiful bras, Noelle has literally taken the load off her back. "I feel lighter," she reports. "My clothes fit so differently, and I can actually see my waist."

Not only is a correctly sized bra more comfortable, but it also offers more lift and support. Instead of relying on the straps of the bra to keep those heavy knockers lifted (which results in those painful indentations), it's the correct sized band and underwire cup that do the heavy lifting. And the further away your boobs are from your stomach, the closer they are to heaven.

GET SOME SUPPORT

As Noelle experienced, the right fitting bra is a game changer—not only in just changing how clothes fit but also in how your body feels. But finding the right bra can be a bit intimidating, so I've solicited help from an expert.

Linda Lewis spent over twenty years working at the corporate headquarters of some of the largest intimate apparel brands. Her last role before retiring was "Senior Manager for National Fit Initiatives," where she traveled across the country training bra fitters. She wrote the training manual on how to get the perfect fit in a bra and shared a few of her tips:

#1 GET FITTED BY AN EXPERT

I know I said this earlier, but I can't reiterate it enough: get fitted by an expert. Bras are an investment. To make sure you're spending your money wisely, seek professional help. An expert bra fitter can assess your size and your needs so you actually enjoy putting on a bra each morning.

Linda said she used to ask every customer two critical questions at the start of each fitting:

1. Does your bra leave red marks anywhere on your body when you take it off?
2. Does your bra pinch you under the arms or around your breasts?

"If it doesn't feel right, it probably isn't," she advised. "The right bra means there's no bulging, no gaps, and no pinching. Pain is not a necessary evil." Amen, Linda.

Some brands offer over eighty different sizes, and most department stores carry a ton of different brands and styles. There's no way you can know your best options without getting assistance. And while bra sizes don't vary *as* much as clothes, a 32G in one brand might not fit as well as the same size in another brand. It could be the shape of the cup, the fabric, or a variation in size. That's why it's critical to ask for assistance and try every bra on before you purchase.

Within bra sizing, there is some wiggle room called "Sister Sizing." For example, in my favorite bra, I wear a 34D. When I went to stock back up, they were out of my size, so my bra fitter recommended I try a 36C and it fit just fine. But again, do not play with size variation without first being fitted!

#2 YOU NEED AT LEAST THREE EVERYDAY BRAS

According to Linda, at the bare minimum, your bra wardrobe needs to consist of the following:

- The bra you're wearing today.
- The bra you had on yesterday.
- The bra you have in the wash.

The spandex and fabric that hold up your boobs need a chance to snap-back after each wear, so *do not* wear the same bra every day. This stretchy, expensive fabric technology gets ruined without proper care. So when Linda says "in the wash," she means "hand-wash or in a mesh laundry bag that you then allow to air dry." Seriously, *do not* put any of your bras in the dryer. That's the fastest way to waste money.

This basic bra wardrobe should consist of everyday, smooth-coverage bras that don't show through thinner fabrics. But a complete assortment of bras includes:

- Lacy bras for when you're feeling frisky.
- Sports bras for your workout regimen.
- A plunge bra for deep necklines.
- A balconette when you need an extra boost.
- A supportive strapless that stays up all night.

By having a bra drawer with options, you're ready for any occasion and can avoid the dreaded moment of "Ugh, why didn't anyone tell me my bra was showing before we took that photo?"

Because bras aren't cheap (at least they shouldn't be if they're actually doing what they are meant to do), one of my money-saving tips is once I get fitted by an expert and have worn those bras for a while to ensure they're comfortable, I then check out discount stores for the same brand.

Of course, I always try the bra on before I leave the store, keeping in mind Linda's tips. But because I know my accurate size and the brands that work for me, I can get deals on the bras I won't wear as frequently as my "everyday" ones.

#3 BRAS CAN BE ALTERED

Shocking, right? When I bought that 36C, the genius at the lingerie boutique told me that in about six months or so, the band might stretch and get too loose. When that happens, I was to come back and get the band tightened. That means they literally cut the band down a few inches based on my rib-cage size.

I once bought a beautiful balconette bra. But because of the fancy lace and the placement of the underwire, the middle of my chest between my breasts would get irritated after a few hours. The same bra store had one of their Fairy Godmothers hand-sew pieces of felt on the back of that middle area. Now I can wear that beauty all day—a major perk of bra specialty boutiques.

Other alterations can be to add a hook and eye extension to the underband or adding additional support to the cups or straps. These fixes can vary in price and feasibility, but remember, the care of your breasts is a critical investment.

SHAPING UP

Putting on a quality, well-fitting and pretty bra each morning must be part of your self-care regimen. You and your boobs deserve to be supported and preserved. Bras not only honor your femininity but also enhance whatever clothing you choose to wear on top. The same goes for shapewear.

Shapewear is a huge industry that sometimes sends an underlying message that your body needs to be sucked and snatched to be beautiful. While I appreciate a smooth base layer under my clothes, I try hard not to feed into unrealistic body standards. Very few women naturally have perky, shapely breasts, an itty-bitty waist, slim thighs, and a curvy butt. No number of bras and girdles can re-create that impossible standard.

Because I am so passionate about bras, I get asked all the time about shapewear. But my opinion on "to Spanx or not to Spanx" might surprise you: I don't care what shapewear you wear—as long you're comfortable and I can't see them.

I have some clients who never leave the house without support over their tummies or bums. A girdle or shaper is part of their everyday attire. I, on the other hand, only wear them for super special occasions, i.e., when I'm going out "fishing for men" in a tight dress. But even when I do have them on, it's a modest amount of support, still allowing me to breathe comfortably. I swear, the few times I've put on a "serious" shaper, I had the worst stomachache, thereby defeating the entire purpose of the dress. Bubble guts aren't fun or sexy.

> My saddlebags are why Spanx exist! Now that I have a baby, I also have a muffin top.
>
> – SARA BLAKELY

When it comes to shapewear, *comfort* is the keyword. Wear whatever feels most comfortable for you. If you feel more comfortable and confident totally sucked in, then lock and load everything up. If you're comfortable with a little bit of jiggle in favor of being able to eat, drink, and be merry, then choose a lighter option.

Whichever you choose (and not choosing is also an option), just make sure you don't have any visible panty lines, muffin tops, or exposed shapewear. While shapewear is supposed to make your body "look sexier," there's *nothing* sexy about beige bike-shorts peeking out under a too-short dress.

Should you choose to make shapewear part of your wardrobe, I have a few suggestions:

#1 PICK YOUR TARGET

So many options exist for shapewear that it can be overwhelming to know what you need for your body. Start with the body part you'd like to "control:

- **Tummy**: Look for a shaping bodysuit or slimming camisole. These are great for eliminating a muffin top. If you're looking for serious support or are postpartum, a waist cincher (i.e. a corset) is suggested. High-rise briefs, thongs, or shorts also work. These bottoms usually come all the way up to your bra, smoothing the mid-section.
- **Arms**: To reduce the jiggling, try a bolero-style arm shaper. Some even come in cute prints and colors to look like an intentional layer under a sleeveless top or dress.
- **Hips & Butt**: Shaper shorts or leggings help to reduce saddlebags as well as the annoying feeling of your thighs rubbing together. Just make sure the shorts don't start to creep up your thighs when you walk. Worst feeling ever. I also love a good slip to hide any cellulite dimples. If you're looking to build up your bum, try butt-lifting shorts that push up and add some curves.
- **All-Over**: Full body slips or bodysuits with shorts give the biggest, all-over bang for your buck. Some have built-in bras, but I prefer that you choose the open bust ones that fit just under your expertly fitted bra. These pieces usually have sculpting in the core and control over the thighs.

#2 CHOOSE YOUR LEVEL

Some days or some dresses might require more support than others. Or sometimes the fabric of a garment is too thin and you just need an extra layer of coverage. Keep your needs (and pain tolerance) in mind when selecting between medium, firm, or extra firm support. Most garments explicitly mention the level, but, in general, the thicker the fabric, the more intense the shaping. Sheerer fabrics like pantyhose or silkier fabrics like a slip are lighter in coverage.

#3 STICK TO YOUR SIZE

As I said earlier, no one knows the size of your clothes, but they do know when something doesn't fit. In the case of shapewear, no one will know your size, but *you* will feel when it doesn't fit; that feeling is a slow death by suffocation. Shapewear already has shape-shifting properties built into each garment, so there's no need to go down a size to "really do something." Instead, just pick a different level of support.

Can the right shapewear help a decent-fitting dress look even better? Absolutely. Can shapewear substitute for the wrong size or not getting alterations? Absolutely not. Shapewear, just like bras and clothes, is meant to enhance, not change. Whether it's going up a size, working with a Fairy Godmother, or updating your lingerie drawer, do whatever you need to do to look, and therefore feel, your best.

No matter what you do, always remember nothing's wrong with your body, and it doesn't need to change.

WORTHY WRAP-UP

1. Choose to be happy with your body today instead of waiting for "The Day."

2. Regardless of what you may not like about your body, be grateful it's keeping you alive.

3. Don't give up on finding clothes you love. If at first you don't succeed, keep trying on clothes until you do.

4. Your boobs deserve to be supported. Get fitted and update your bra wardrobe.

5. Shapewear is a choice: choose whatever makes you feel most comfortable.

WORTHY WORDS

Body, I appreciate you and I love you.

PART TWO

PRETTY AND PROFESSIONAL

CHAPTER 6

PINK AND BLUE

———

"Makeup and fashion are for girls who aren't smart like you."

Growing up in a household with two highly educated professional parents, I heard variations of the above phrase. At an early age, I concluded that I had to make a choice between being smart and being pretty. And with my parents, the only option was the former.

Academics were highly prized in my house. Books were everywhere, with my parents often hosting monthly book club meetings. I was an only child, so their parties were my parties too. I would sit in the living room listening and sometimes even participating in the discussions. Some of my favorite memories as a child were debating with my lawyer father about politics or worldly affairs. We felt a great sense of pride in being a "smart" family.

On a daily basis, I was told to focus on my studies, be the smartest one in the room, focus on being a "strong" leader, and leave the lipstick and outfits to the superficial "girly girls." Yes, my mother loves to shop (and my dad is also a secret bargain shopper), but our shopping trips were about the enjoyment of clothes, the accumulation of things my parents never had, and mainly about our perceived need to always look "presentable." Pretty was never the focus.

This idea that my only choice was to be smart and not pretty further fueled my tomboy wardrobe of sweatpants. While priding myself on being one of the hardest working and smartest people in the classroom, I began to look down on the pretty girly girls, automatically assuming they were ditzes solely because they wore pink and ruffles.

I carried this negative correlation between intelligence and beauty throughout college and into the workplace. When I got my first job on the Old Navy Men's merchandising team, I justified my menswear-inspired uniform of jeans and tee shirts as my way of being taken seriously, much to my mother's dismay. At the young age of twenty-three, I was managing a multi-million-dollar men's polo shirt business. In my mind, my wardrobe seemed trivial.

PULL YOURSELF TOGETHER

After I left corporate America, I realized two things:

1. My mother is always right.
2. "Pretty" isn't frivolous or only for bimbos.

When I became an entrepreneur, I finally realized that being "pretty" meant using my wardrobe and image to stand out from the crowd, become the face of my business, and own my femininity to connect with other women. Those practices would have increased my "executive presence" and ultimately served me well in my former jobs.

Sylvia Ann Hewlett is one of the world's most influential business thinkers. She wrote *the* book on Executive Presence. In her book, aptly titled *Executive Presence*, Sylvia and her team interviewed hundreds of senior executives on different components of executive presence. Their data suggests that a successful professional image is more about effort than genes.

> More than a third of the senior executives in our survey (men and women) considered "polish and grooming" vital to men's and women's Executive Presence (EP), whereas less than a fifth said that physical attractiveness matters. It turns out that the intrinsic stuff (body type, height) is not what matters most; rather it's what you do with what you've got. As one leader put it in an interview, "You've got to look as though you tried, that you pulled yourself together."[19]

Despite the conventional cultural definition of "pretty" equating to whiteness and thinness, for the purpose of this book, pretty is about showing up as your best self. If you think you're not pretty, I'm here to tell you that as a matter of mindset and effort, pretty is available to all of us. Owning my "pretty" wasn't about being provocative or relying on my looks to get ahead. It was about realizing that first impressions matter.

---

19 Sylvia Ann Hewlett, *Executive Presence: The Missing Link Between Merit and Success* (New York: Harper Business, 2014), 82.

A variety of studies have proven that first impressions are made in mere seconds. Many of them are based on facial features and expressions, but one study assessed the impact clothing has on a first impression.

In the study, participants had five seconds to assess faceless images of a man on five dimensions: confidence, success, trustworthiness, salary, and flexibility. One image depicted a man wearing a bespoke (made-to-measure) suit. The other image featured a regular (off-the-rack) suit, similar in color. Impressions arose only from clothing and were not confounded by physical attractiveness or facial features. The man pictured in the bespoke suit was rated more positively on practically all attributes. The study concludes that even minor clothing manipulations can give rise to significantly different assumptions about the wearer.[20]

If people can judge so much about a man based solely on a navy suit, imagine how much impact our clothing choices have as women. Confidence, level of success, and trustworthiness are all critical factors when determining whether to do business with someone.

By investing time, effort, and money into my image, I was also investing in my business. To be taken seriously as a professional and successful business owner, I had to take my own self-image seriously by looking the part and creating my own version of pretty.

---

20   Neil Howlett, "The Influence of Clothing on First Impressions," *Journal of Fashion Marketing and Management: An International Journal* 17, no. 1 (2013): 38-48.

DON'T PLAY SMALL

Had I known then what I know now, I would have applied these same principles during my corporate career. But peer pressure and the voices in our head can be very influential in getting us to do things differently.

While the need to "blend in and play small" in the workplace is rarely said explicitly, it's definitely felt and internalized by many women. Carla, now a forty-two-year-old executive in technology, recalled how her first weeks in her new developer job influenced her wardrobe:

> When I started my career in technology, I was very young. Because of my age and because there weren't very many women in technology and certainly not very many women of color, I felt like I was always trying to prove myself. I explicitly remember no one was taking me seriously as a developer. One of my [male] coworkers admitted to me years later, "You know, when you first walked into the office, I thought, *"There's no way she's going to be a good developer"*, just looking at you in your high heels and fancy shirts."

> He assumed I wouldn't be a good developer because I didn't initially "look the part." The visual model of a female developer back then was frumpy, wearing black, grey, and padded shoes; short hair, no makeup, and glasses. I was "too attractive" and "put together" to be considered a good developer. I think because I was aware of the perception of what a female in technology looked like and wanted to feel accepted, I

started to dress down in a lot of gray and a lot of black, which is really not my personality.

I've interviewed women in tech, banking, medicine, finance, academia, and even refrigeration, and across these industries, there's this contradiction of women needing to be presentable but never *pretty*. The image of leadership and what it means to have "executive presence" is usually dominated by masculine suits or boring basics.

We're expected to look like leaders who just happen to be women instead of owning our femininity and personal style. While many companies applaud forward-thinking strategies and an entrepreneurial spirit, many female employees feel pressured to blend in and play small regarding their image.

Even if it makes others uncomfortable, I will love who I am.

– JANELLE MONÁE

We are always supposed to look like we tried, but not *too* hard. We don't want to make anyone else feel uncomfortable about their own appearance. Heaven forbid we get the, "Wow, you look nice today. You must be interviewing somewhere else" remark from a nosy co-worker. Nor can we put too much effort into our appearance, lest we be judged as superficial or stupid.

Like me, so many women fall victim to the ridiculous cultural belief that it's impossible for a woman to be both intelligent and attractive. This leaves many of us succumbing to uninspired and invisible wardrobes like Carla's uniform.

FIND YOUR PINK

Last year, a famous fast-food chain hired me to speak to thirty young women who were being trained to become franchisees. The grueling work of being on your feet all day in a kitchen full of hot grease made wardrobe building a challenge. After my presentation, where I suggested ways to still look the part of a restaurant owner without sacrificing style, a beautiful curvy blonde named Nikki asked a question that stuck with me. "As you can probably tell, the thirty of us women are the minority in this training program. The rest of the 250 trainees are men," she noted. "When I'm working with my team members on group projects, I always feel the need to wear blazers and masculine clothes, even though I don't feel comfortable in them. What should I do?"

"Why are you wearing clothes you don't feel good in?" I countered.

"Because some of these guys treat me like the secretary, asking me to take the notes for the meeting and even getting them coffee," Nikki confided. "My hope is that by wearing these blazers, they will treat me like one of them and respect me more."

My heart broke when I saw many other young women nodding in agreement. Trying to hold my sadness and anger in,

I replied, "First, let me say how sad I am that, as a twenty-two-year-old woman in the twenty-first century, you're still experiencing this. Secondly, I'll give you a tip about men. The kind of guy who will treat you like the secretary because you're a woman is the kind of asshole who will always treat you like a secretary, no matter what you're wearing." I continued, "My goal is to help you build a wardrobe that you feel confident in. If pleated skirts and florals make you feel amazing, I want you to rock the hell outta that pink and purple. So much so that the next time he asks you to get his coffee, you feel powerful enough to tell him to get his own." The older female mentors cheered me on.

I don't think being beautiful takes away from your credibility.

–SOLEDAD O'BRIEN

While pink might be Nikki's power color of choice, Nancy relies on red to make a statement. Every time I see Nancy at a networking event, I notice her—partly because she's tall but mainly because of the red suit or blazer she's always wearing. When I interviewed her for this book, Nancy let me in on her "code red." She explained, "As a corporate trainer, I've had to lead mostly-male audiences, some of whom have challenged me and questioned my authority. I had to find a strategic way to let them know that's not what you want to do with me. So I started to wear red, the ultimate power color, to command the room. Now, over 50 percent of my closet is red. It's my color."

Choosing to wear red might be a big step for some of us, but wearing a pink cardigan instead of a black blazer or bright green instead of toned-down grey is definitely do-able. And as insignificant as these choices seem, the way we choose to dress for work can have a huge impact on how we behave and how we feel about ourselves. I hoped Nikki would start owning her pretty and that, by doing so, she would feel empowered to stand up to coworkers trying to bully her.

THE BLACKS AND BLUES

By being Nikki's wake up call, I hope I saved her the years of Invisible Wardrobe Worry that plagued me and Carla into playing small. My wake-up call to executive presence was becoming an entrepreneur. For Carla, one of her consulting clients had asked if she had anything other than grey in her closet.

During my interview with bright and bubbly Meagan, she shared that her wardrobe revelation came from her seventy-two-year-old white male Thermal Engineering SVP, proving that Divine Intervention can come from anywhere.

Within the first few minutes on the phone with Meagan, I could sense her infectiously fun energy. Like me and Carla, Meagan succumbed to the pressure of dressing down to match her surroundings, donning an Invisible Wardrobe of black pants and blue polos, the "feminine" version of her fellow male engineers' khakis and polos. "Wearing those black and blues never matched my personality," Meagan recalled. And after just a few minutes on the phone with her, I agreed with that 100 percent.

"But not only did they just not match my personality, those blacks and blues started to impact the way I interacted at work," Meagan revealed. "I began to take on this very serious personality that was very different than who I really was. As I started to move up the ranks and get promoted, I started getting invited to more social situations where things were happening outside of work, like dinners and holiday parties at the home of the executives. I started showing up there in my regular "off duty" clothes and my "regular" personality."

"What were your regular clothes?" I asked.

"Bright, colorful, lots of patterns, and I would wear these bright colors with gold high heels and big hair. The surprising thing was these executives liked that version better. They would say things like, 'Oh my gosh, you're so funny.' And I would say, 'Yes, of course I'm funny.' And they would reply, 'But you never show it at work.' And they were right. I didn't even realize how much I was turning myself on and off, all stemming from those blacks and blues."

Meagan continued, "Ever since college, I was told that as a black female engineer, I would be the 'only one' and that 'they,' the majority, won't understand you, so you have to be like them, act like them, and dress like them. For so long, I was the 'safe black girl' who my coworkers and executives liked but didn't really know. On a Monday after one of those parties, an old white man, one of the SVP's, came into my office and gave me a suggestion that changed the game: 'Just be you.' 'Yeah, this is me,' I replied. 'No, no, no, no. I've *seen* you. She's pretty cool. Bring her to work when you come in on Tuesday.'"

By showing up as her true self, in wardrobe and personality, Meagan was finally invited into "The Boy's Club" that she couldn't get into years before. "What was so interesting is that by assimilating, even though they didn't know what it was, these leaders knew something about me wasn't quite trustworthy. They were right. I was hiding so much of myself. When they finally got to know the real me, they said, 'Wow, that's a lot but cool, we'll take it.' And I was finally accepted."

Acceptance from others won't happen until we first accept ourselves.

By choosing to wear whatever makes you feel "pretty," you show those around you that you're proud of who you are and what you bring to the table.

WORTHY WRAP-UP

1. Pretty and smart aren't mutually exclusive. Give yourself permission to be both.
2. No matter what industry you're in or the level you're at, having executive presence is critical. Enhance yours by pulling yourself together.
3. Pretty is a choice. Own yours and invest in a wardrobe that reflects your version of pretty.

WORTHY WORDS

I am pretty, smart, and powerful.

CHAPTER 7

THE HERO'S JOURNEY

———

Meagan's story is one I've heard and seen so many times from clients and interviewees for this book. Their journeys of reaching professional success usually went something like this:

- **Step 1**: Be the smartest, hardest working person on the team. Outwork everyone so that your merits always outweigh the biases that come from being a woman or a woman of color.
- **Step 2**: While you're busy working hard, fight against the "typical stereotypes" by downplaying anything that could draw attention to your gender or your race, including, but not limited to, feminine clothing, makeup, hair, tone of voice, personality, and mannerisms.
- **Step 3**: Create multiple personalities: an on-duty self and off-duty self. Exhaust yourself trying to keep the two from ever crossing paths.
- **Step 4**: Receive the big promotions, credibility, and financial success while also isolating yourself from your peers.
- **Step 5**: Once you've "made it" and it's "safe," then let loose a little bit, let your hair down (literally and figuratively), and show more of who you really are.

"Playing the game," as Cheryl, a black sixty-year-old executive explained, was how things had to be done in the era of desegregation and the women's liberation movement. "We didn't have the luxury of being ourselves when we were first starting out. We had to play by the rules of the white men in charge in order to get ahead."

I met Terry while I was facilitating a workshop at the Mercedes-Benz corporate office. Standing at all of 4'9", Terry is a petite but powerful force of energy. After the workshop, she shared with me her illustrious career path in the auto industry. Only then did it sink in for me that, not long ago, things were very different for women of all races.

Ideally, I want to see all beauties, all shapes, all sizes, all skin tones, all backgrounds represented in my profession. Now that I am blessed to be that reflection I was once looking for, I'm making a promise to speak out for that little girl that I used to be.

—DANIELLE BROOKS

As a white woman in the automobile industry climbing the ranks in the 1980s, Terry's wardrobe consisted of skirt suits with boxy blazers and collared blouses with cross-over bows, emulating a man's suit and tie. "Well, what did the women in leadership wear?" I asked. Terry's response blew me away, "Morgan, there were no women in leadership back then." Whoa.

While there is no question that racism, sexism, and homophobia are still very rampant in our society and in the workplace, a tide is changing. A new era of expression and individuality is here. At age thirty-six, I am incredibly indebted to the sacrifices the women of previous generations made for me. Without their willingness to break barriers and be "the first" and "the only" at their universities and companies, I wouldn't have the freedom to express myself and encourage you to do the same.

APPROPRIATELY AUTHENTIC

As scary as it might be to wear the pink cardigan, gains can be made by strategically standing out from the crowd. A series of studies completed at Harvard University and later published in the *Journal of Consumer Research* explored how people reacted when someone broke established dress norms only slightly. In one scenario, a man wearing a red bow tie at a black-tie affair was viewed as having higher status and competence than the men who wore a black bow tie. In another example, the researchers found that when a female professor wore red Converse sneakers while giving a lecture, audience members rated her with high status and competence, proving that we humans value uniqueness.[21]

The results suggest that since non-conformity has a social cost, observers usually infer that a nonconforming individual

---

21 Matthew Hutson, "Dress for Success," *Scientific American Mind* 27, no. 1 (2015): 13.

is in a powerful position that allows her to risk the social costs of nonconformity without fear of losing her place in the social hierarchy.[22]

This means that by wearing that pink cardigan or floral dress in a sea of all black, your boss, teammates, and clients will assume that because you were "brave" enough to stand out, you're also powerful enough to absorb the "risk."

By being grounded in your worthiness, you're confident about what you bring to the table, so you're not desperate for approval, which is the ultimate power move.

It's important to note that these examples of a red sneaker or a pink cardigan are still appropriate. This is *not* about rebelling against the dress code by wearing pajamas or having your boobs out. It's about showing that you know the rules of the game but have found a way to put your own spin on the rule book.

Being aware of and considerate to the culture of each environment is paramount before any fashion statement. But

22 Silvia Bellezza, "The Red Sneakers Effect: Inferring Status and Competence from Signals of Nonconformity," *Journal of Consumer Research* 41, no. 1 (2014): 35-54.

by being "appropriately authentic" and making intentional statements with your wardrobe, not only do you feel more powerful and confident, but people around you see you as a leader, a leader who isn't afraid to be herself. It's this type of confidence and authenticity that people want to be around, even in the "Good Ole Boy's Club" that eluded Meagan for years.

> In order to be irreplaceable, one must always be different.
>
> – COCO CHANEL

SETTING THE STANDARD

According to the 2019 Women in the Workplace Study, which surveyed 389 companies and thirteen million employees, women comprise only 21 percent of C-suite leadership, with women of color only 5 percent.[23] This means about one in five C-suite executives is a woman and one in twenty-five is a woman of color. Representation matters. The more women in power show up as their whole, authentic, pretty selves, the less afraid young women like Nikki are of owning their femininity.

Based on the aforementioned study, my own journey, and the tinge of regret I heard in Carla's and Meagan's stories,

---

23   Rachel Thomas et al., "Women in the Workplace 2019," *Lean In*, (2019): 6.

I want to propose a new hero's journey for women in the workplace:

- **Step 1**: Be the smartest, hardest working person on the team.
- **Step 2**: While working hard, make sure to show that you're more than a worker bee. Take the time away from work to invest in your image and personality. Find the clothes, hairstyles, and mannerisms that show your version of "pretty" while still being appropriate for the company culture.
- **Step 3**: Build authentic connections. Command respect by honoring yourself and image while giving others permission to be their best self.
- **Step 4**: Receive the big promotions, credibility, and financial success that you enjoy and can be proud of.
- **Step 5**: Once you've "made it," share the gospel of living in your purpose and owning who you are with the younger generations. Change the tide.

Don't ever underestimate the importance you can have because history has shown us that courage can be contagious…

−MICHELLE OBAMA

"Aunt" Marianne Williamson reminds us of our purpose with this: "And as we let our own light shine, we unconsciously give other people permission to do the same. As we are liberated from our own fear, our presence automatically liberates others."[24] Let's free ourselves from the past and start lighting the way for the women who come after us. Just as women like Cheryl and Terry blazed the trail to the C-Suite by being a beacon of light, we, too, can continue to make strides in diversity for the next generation.

PRETTY PROFESSIONAL

What's your version of the red bow tie or red Converse sneakers? Finding and owning your pretty doesn't have to be, nor should it be, extreme. This isn't about too-short dresses, or blatantly disrespecting company dress code or common sense. This is about finding ways to show individuality and uniqueness in your style that makes you memorable and authentic.

A few "Pretty Professional" tips:

- Choose red or any other color shoe that makes a statement. My personal favorite is leopard.
- Add jewelry: Layers of pearls, bold costume jewelry, and brooches all add a touch of flair to any outfit. Just make sure to only wear one statement piece at a time.
- Try interesting color combinations and prints. Try an orange blouse with a camel sweater and navy pants. Or try a black and white polka-dotted top with black and white striped pants.
- Don a vest or polished and fitted leather jacket instead of a blazer or cardigan.

---

24   Williamson, *A Return to Love.*

- Give your legs some air in a dress or skirt instead of always relying on black pants.
- Have a signature (but current) hairstyle, nail color, or lipstick.

None of these items are "harder" or less comfortable to wear than those blacks, blues, and grey's Carla and Meagan were wearing. But these items do take a bit of intentional shopping and the confidence to wear them.

THE IMPRESSION OF INCREASE

The notion of standing out from the crowd doesn't just apply to climbing the corporate ladder. The importance of image and owning one's pretty is just as important to entrepreneurs and those of us in traditional sales roles.

When my mother first started her career in life insurance, she remembered the company CEO telling the sales team, "If we're going to ask someone for a million-dollar life insurance policy, we need to look like a million dollars and like we can handle a million dollars." Looking like a million bucks doesn't mean dripping in diamonds and designers. It means looking like you've done several million-dollar deals (even if you haven't *yet)*.

In the 1910 landmark guide to wealth creation, *The Science of Getting Rich: Your Master Key to Success,* Wallace D. Wattles outlines specific practices that ensure personal and financial success, one of which is always giving the impression of increase.

And in so far as your business consists of dealing with other men...the key-thought of all your efforts must be to convey to their minds the impression of increase. Increase is what all men and all women are seeking; it is the urge of the Formless Intelligence [God] within them, seeking fuller expression...And because it is the deepest instinct of their natures, all men and women are attracted to him who can give them more of the means of life. You must so impress others that they will feel that in associating with you they will get an increase for themselves.[25]

Any Sales 101 book will tell you that sales isn't about pushing a product on someone. Sales is about building relationships and creating win-win situations for all involved. As a saleswoman (and to be honest, even if you don't think your job is sales, you're always selling yourself and your ideas), it's your job to communicate how your product or service will advance the lives of others.

No matter what you're selling, you're not selling a product; you're selling improvement, health, happiness, peace of mind, advancement, and increase. Your image needs to give that impression as well. After all, I bet you wouldn't trust your life savings to a financial adviser who looked like she didn't have any money herself.

When I took the leap of faith and became a full-time entrepreneur, my wardrobe changed immediately. The women

---

25   Wallace D. Wattles, *The Science of Getting Rich: Your Master Key to Success* (Blacksburg: Thrifty Books, 2009), 50-51.

I wanted to work with were high-performing profession-als, typically in more conservative industries. My former "corporate business casual" uniform of jeans and basic sweaters wouldn't cut it. I needed my image to convey that I understood their image challenges and could pro-vide solutions.

I feel more confident and at peace with who I am and am more aware of what I bring to the table, but that was a huge journey. When you find you, really find you, that's when everything starts falling into place.

—JENNIFER LOPEZ

My wardrobe became dressier than ever. For every network-ing opportunity or speaking engagement, I wore a statement dress or a pleated skirt with a bright blouse. High heels replaced the flats. I've had several clients tell me that they chose to work with me over another stylist because they knew they could trust me with their image based on how I cared for my own. But wardrobe choices aren't important just for image consultants like me.

Last summer, I presented one of my Executive Style work-shops to a group of women at a sales conference. Most of the women were in pharmaceutical, insurance, and financial sales, and my presentation focused on sharpening their image to increase their revenue.

> ## *No matter your profession, your image can still have a direct impact on your income.*

After the workshop, gorgeous, curvy, plus-sized Jonella revealed to me that she was stuck in a style rut, which was confirmed by the basic black dress she was wearing. I encouraged her to break up with the black and start experimenting with color, as she was way too pretty to be playing small.

Fast forward to three months later, when she agreed to chat with me for this book. Not only was Jonella wearing a "superhero" blue fitted wrap dress and chili pepper red flats, but her whole aura radiated confidence. She shared with me what had changed:

> That conference, and you in particular, Morgan, were literally part of my transformation. I knew I had to stop getting in my own way and start showing up as my best self. I started examining my strengths and remembered anther sales rep telling me, "Your high energy is intoxicating."
>
> I applied your instructions to wear color and I now wear red all the time to match my energy. Since

I started wearing color, it's literally like a fire hose has been turned on. Everywhere I go, the post office, the grocery store, folks are stopping me. "Oh my god, I love that color on you." or "Where did you get those red shoes?" My confidence has soared, and it's changed the way I interact with the doctors I work with. Now I'm not afraid to be direct and have more fun with them. My sales numbers are literally through the roof.

People do business with people who appear to be successful. And in Jonella's case, her bright new wardrobe clearly gave the impression of increase. Her decision to wear colors as bold as red, cobalt, and hot pink became part of her personal brand and signified to her clients that she, and therefore her product, is worthy of attention and investment.

CROWN YOURSELF

After every one of my presentations, it never fails that a woman in the audience asks me what hairstyles and makeup applications are deemed "professional." I especially get questions from black women about their hair. A question like "what will people think if I wear my hair in braids?" is more about permission than professionalism. Just as there have been so many unspoken "rules" about wardrobe choices, there are many pressures to conform when it comes to beauty.

Due to subtle and (not so subtle) judgments, black women need legal protection to wear their hair as it grows out of their head. In 2020, The C.R.O.W.N (Create a Respectful and Open

Workplace for Natural Hair) Act was passed in California and New York to ensure protection against discrimination based on hairstyles by extending statutory protection to hair texture and protective styles in the Fair Employment and Housing Act and state Education Codes.[26]

> # Caring for myself is not self-indulgence, it is self-preservation, and that is an act of political warfare.

> – AUDRE LORDE

In the year 2020. It's no wonder so many black women are not sure what's deemed "professional." They've been brainwashed into thinking something is wrong with their hair.

It's time to change that narrative. My advice is as long as you look like you've "pulled yourself together," wear your hair however you feel pretty. There's something to be said about using your hair as part of your "brand" and creating a consistent look, but if switching it up gives you the confidence you need to start each day feeling like a boss, keep your options open.

---

26 Crown Coalition, "The Official Campaign of the CROWN Act," accessed on May 17th, 2020.

No matter what color, texture, or style you choose for your hair, consider what you want to be known for and if your hair compliments that message.

We are able to transform ourselves, not only how we are perceived, but how we feel.

– BOBBI BROWN

For makeup, the same guideline of "polished and pulled together" applies. During my entire corporate career, I refused to wear makeup, thinking it was too "frivolous." I wish I had known then what I know now. A little bit of lip gloss and concealer would go a long way in signaling that I made an effort.

Research conducted at Harvard Medical School concludes that compared to a bare face, women with makeup were judged as more competent, likable, attractive, and trust-worthy.[27] This does not mean you need to spend hours each morning contouring your cheekbones unless that's the most enjoyable part of your morning routine. A "five-minute face" of light concealer or foundation, blush, and a lipstick that brings you joy will help to convey the "Impression of Increase."

---

27 Nancy L. Etcoff, "Cosmetics as a Feature of the Extended Human Phe-notype: Modulation of the Perception of Biologically Important Facial Signals," *Plos* 6, no. 10 (2011).

Makeup and hair are meant to enhance the beautiful woman you are. Do not succumb to the pressure of totally transforming into someone else. Instead, find an authentic, sustainable look for your lifestyle. While you're honoring your prettiness in the morning, channel those famous L'Oréal commercials and say to yourself, "Because I'm worth it."

MIND OVER MATTER

As an overworked professional or an entrepreneur, it can be incredibly easy to put your image on the back burner. So many other demands and tasks require our attention. Projects need to be completed, teams need to be managed, invoices needed to be sent, and new clients need to be secured. But none of that can happen when we're not operating at our optimum.

Humans are equally mind, body, and spirit. In our careers, so many of us women rely completely on our minds, totally neglecting our spirits and our bodies. This results in burnout, job dissatisfaction, and, for some of us, serious stress-induced health problems. By honoring our bodies through our wardrobes, our soul and personality can shine through, making our work more enjoyable and successful.

Will dressing better cure your high blood pressure? No. But starting to care about what you wear to work each morning will motivate you to start caring about how you treat your body.

> *Investing in a Powerfully Pretty wardrobe will also give you the confidence to set better work-life boundaries, ask for the raise, or land the big client, all of which will make life a little easier.*

Building a professional wardrobe isn't about hiding behind "power suits" but about allowing the pretty within you to help you achieve your professional goals.

WORTHY WRAP-UP

1. You are the hero of your professional success. Use your wardrobe to help you get there.
2. Discover what Powerfully Pretty elements you want to add to your wardrobe and rock the hell outta them.
3. Always convey the impression of increase.
4. Honor your inherent beauty with whatever hairstyle and makeup feels good to you.
5. Your purpose and your profession deserve your whole self—mind, body, and spirit.

WORTHY WORDS

Investing in my pretty increases my power and influence.

CHAPTER 8

SEXY

—

From the moment I met Alexis, I envied her.

We met at a networking event for lawyers, real estate agents, and accountants three years ago. I was just starting to grow my business and would attend all events where my ideal client of professional women would be.

Not to toot my own horn, but as a stylist, I know how to use my wardrobe as a networking asset. And at these types of events, I was usually the best dressed in a room full of boring black suits. In my distinctive green-and-blue-striped Missoni sweater dress and brand-new nude pumps, tonight was no exception. But as blisters began to form from the new shoes, I started to feel self-conscious of my "painful shoe hobble" and was ready to go home.

As I circled the room, I saw a tall woman with short hair in a black fitted dress holding court. A crowd of adoring men circled around her as she discussed her real estate business. Even if those men were gathered for other reasons, this woman captivated her audience as she demonstrated her superior knowledge of the industry, responded to questions, and shared her perspective on the market.

It was wonderful to observe Alexis's magnetic charisma. I looked down at my colorful dress and Satan Stilettos and felt silly compared to her chic and simple black dress. I instantly thought, "Man, I want her to be my best friend." When a mutual friend introduced us, in my stupor I blurted out, "I think we should be BFFs." With her infectious laugh, Alexis said, "Okay then, what's your name, my new BFF?"

Since our meeting, Alexis and I have begun to build our friendship, meeting several times for drinks, birthday parties, and brunches. Wherever we go, men flock to Alexis. It's fascinating to watch her coyly flirt while graciously declining any unwanted advances. "Sex sells," Alexis unapologetically explained to me over martinis. "In the real estate world, there's a fine line to be walked. I never downplay my looks, but I always play to my audience. If I'm going to a happy hour with mostly men, I'll wear something fitted but never revealing."

Being strong is very sexy.

−SANAA LATHAN

Sex "selling" isn't new news. Practically every magazine ad or TV commercial, whether it's lipstick, luggage, or laundry detergent, somehow relies on sexiness to make us want the product. But *why?*

An article in *Psychology Today* confirms what Alexis already knows: "Sexual attraction goes further than just staring...it attracts the agent to *act* as well. Sexual desire increases your action readiness...People are more likely to approach a sexy person than a beautiful one. Being sexy is seen as a kind of invitation..."[28]

By using her sex appeal to her advantage, Alexis was inspiring and inviting action—not *that* kind of "action" but the kind that resulted in a sold house and a check. Her sexiness invited people into her circle, allowing her to expand her network, build relationships, and sell more houses.

As someone who has never quite felt comfortable receiving attention from men, I envied Alexis's command of a room and the opposite sex. *What's her secret?* I would ask myself. *What perfume or magic potion is she drinking that turns her into such a siren, attracting any man within a fifty-foot radius? How can I dress more like her and get myself a date?*

THE SCIENCE OF SEXY

Turns out that the sex appeal Alexis oozes doesn't come from her scent or her incredible thrift-store sponsored wardrobe. The same charisma that made me want to be friends with her is the same thing that made her so sexy. Apparently, sexiness is an inside job.

---

28 Aaron Ben-Zeév PhD, "What's More Important, Being Sexy or Being Beautiful?" *Psychology Today,* May 1, 2018.

Every man I've asked has given me practically the same answer to my question "What makes a woman sexy to you?"

"Confidence," they all reply.

I roll my eyes and implore, "Cut the bullshit and be honest. What is it *really*?" Their second answer is the same as their first and the same as that of Professor Aaron Ben-Ze'ev. In that same *Psychology Today* article, he claims that "confidence, honesty, talent, brightness, and good manners are very sexy. This is in accordance with the 'personality halo,' because of high-praiseworthy qualities, such as wisdom, caring, kindness, and social status, the person is perceived to be more appealing." [29]

The simplicity and "woo-woo-ness" of this answer frustrated me. Bright and kind? *That's it?* Hell, I'm both of those (most days), and yet I'm home alone on a Friday night and I don't command a room like Alexis. *Or do I?*

When I look back on the few times of my life when I've felt the most confident, the most like an all-out bad-ass, the most, dare I say, "sexy," those were the moments when I was in my zone. Whether it was giving a keynote speech on stage or meeting someone new at a bar, I was lit up talking about something I'm passionate about.

No matter what I was wearing, I knew I was captivating my audience by what I was saying. I was *telling* my sexiness

---

29 Aaron Ben-Ze'ev PhD, *The Subtlety of Emotions* (Cambridge: MIT Press, 2000), 406-413.

through words and confidence instead of *showing* it through clothes. I'd be willing to bet you've had those moments too, when you're in the zone, killing it at whatever you do best—cooking a great meal, scoring on the basketball ball court, or negotiating a big contract.

I smile a lot, I win a lot, and I'm really sexy.

—SERENA WILLIAMS

So we've been out in the world being sexy and not even realizing it, and definitely not maximizing it to our benefit like Alexis. Why is that?

I've come up with two main reasons why we women have stifled our inherent, natural sex appeal—sales and safety. As they say in all crime documentaries, let's "follow the money" and start with sales.

THE SELLING OF SEXY

In our culture, women have been indoctrinated with the idea that sexiness comes from something we acquire: a new box of hair color or a new set of boobs. According to *Business Insider*, the beauty industry is a 532-billion-dollar industry.[30] *Billion*, with a B, which equates to 532 billion reasons why

---

30   Bethany Biron, "Beauty Has Blown up to Be a $532 Billion Industry—and Analysts Say That These 4 Trends Will Make It Even Bigger," *Business Insider*, Jul 9, 2019.

we're constantly sold products that will make us "desired" by men. Every time we scroll through social media or turn on the TV or open a magazine or peruse the aisles of Target, we're being told, "Buy this and you, too, can become sexy."

This is not to say that there's anything wrong with makeup, hair extensions, or plastic surgery. I have used or have considered using all three and many more of these "enhancers." But whenever and however I dress my face, hair, and body, I consider the real intention behind the choice.

Am I dying my hair blonde because this shade compliments my skin tone or because Euro-American beauty standards compel me to equate lighter hair as better?

Do I like this red lipstick because I feel like a diva with it on or because all my friends are wearing it?

Are these high heels the best choice for my comfort level or am I hoping a man will notice me in them?

With all of my beauty and wardrobe decisions, I try to make sure I'm focused on looking and feeling like the best version of myself instead of trying to look like a substandard copy of someone else. Do I always live up to this ideal? No. Sometimes I just want to shut the place down while looking incredible, even if I can't breathe and have to sit the whole night.

But the irony of those nights is after I do all that primping, hoping to catch the eye of Mr. Right (or Mr. Tonight), the minute I walk into the bar, I'm instantly self-conscious, nervous, and even annoyed if a man stares at me for too long.

Despite looking like a grown-ass woman, inside I'm still that thirteen-year-old girl who hears her mother yelling, "Cover up!" in Burger King.

If I'm 100 percent honest, I still equate sexiness to being scared.

THE SAFETY OF SEXY

In the United States, one in three women experience sexual assault in their lifetime.[31] Based on our country's violent history toward women and people of color, I guess I shouldn't be all that shocked. Nonetheless, for a first-world country, these numbers are staggering. And thanks to the recent #MeToo movement, more and more women are coming forward with their experiences of rape, coercion, unwanted sexual contact, or exposure. Whether it's at work, at home, or just walking down the street, many of us don't feel safe.

When one person says, 'Yeah, me, too,' it gives permission for others to open up.

–TARANA BURKE

Growing up in the rural south during the Civil Rights movement, the women in my family lived in constant fear of attack,

---

31   Sharon G. Smith, "The National Intimate Partner and Sexual Violence Survey (NISVS): 2010-2012 State Report" (Atlanta, GA: National Center for Injury Prevention and Control, Centers for Disease Control and Prevention, 2017), 1.

or worse. That moment in Burger King had less to do with my tank top but more about my mother's past, yet it still influences my own sentiments around attractiveness. Throughout my interviews and client work, I hear story after story of how lacking control over one's body directly impacts the concept of sexiness and wardrobe choices.

After being raped at the age of twelve, Isabelle did the only thing she could think of to ward off unwanted attention from men—gain weight. Courtney's forty-two J-sized chest was so prominent, men were always asking her for hugs, not to be friendly but to cop themselves a feel. People referred to her as "Courtney with the big tits." Veronica started wearing baggy pants exclusively to stop her male investment banking coworkers from commenting about her butt. While waiting for the subway, a teenage Gina was assaulted as a group of teenage boys grabbed her butt and breasts before running away.

To add insult to injury, many of us have experienced "victim blaming," where it's insinuated (or explicitly said) that based on what we were wearing or how we were standing, we must have been "asking for it." We begin to associate sexiness with a loss of safety and start doing whatever we can to regain agency over our bodies. Because of the constant sense of being in danger, some of us try to do everything we can to downplay any visual markers of sex appeal.

But how does one balance protection with pretty? For those of us romantically and sexually interested in men, how can we look visually appealing to the opposite sex while not attracting "the wrong kind" of attention? We're caught in this twisted web of looking like a "good girl that he'll bring home to his mother" without looking like a librarian. But society also tells us (and sells us) that we must look sexy but not like a "slut," which is open to anyone's interpretation. We become so conditioned with these "rules" that we begin to judge other women who don't adhere to them.

SLUT SHAMING

Whether it's a celebrity in a magazine or a woman walking past us on the street, by being another woman's harshest critic, we become the crabs in the barrel, pulling each other down. This practice can be especially damaging when the critique comes from someone we trust.

During her early years in the Air Force, Misty looked to the guidance of a more senior female officer. "Because there were so few women, I really sought out a connection with this woman," Misty recalled. "She became a mentor of mine; someone I could trust since I didn't always feel comfortable with the male officers. One day out of nowhere, she told me, 'Your boobs are way too big and are becoming a distraction to everyone. You're getting a reputation.' I was devastated and confused. We all had uniforms, and I made sure my shirts were fitting me properly and that my bras were supportive. So for her to make this accusatory remark about something I had no control over, it broke me."

When her male boss asked why there were tears in her eyes, she recounted the comment and asked for his feedback. "My commander was just as shocked by that comment as I was," she continued. "He assured me that he hadn't heard any such feedback and was furious at my mentor."

Even all these years later, I can still see the disappointment on Misty's face as she looked back on that time. "That comment stuck with me, making me question everything about myself. It took me years to realize that what she said to me actually had nothing to do with me and was actually her own insecurities. Now that I'm a mentor, I make it a point to never say something that could hurt a young person like that hurt me."

Another woman doing her part in changing how we treat each other is model-turned-women's rights activist Amber Rose. As a voluptuous woman who used to work as a stripper before rising to fame, Amber Rose has been bombarded with harsh critiques of how many men she's allegedly slept with, how she raises her children, or how she runs her businesses, solely based on her image.

In 2017, she founded the Amber Rose SlutWalk protest and women's conference on sex positivity, which aims to take power away from derogatory labels and end rape culture, victim blaming, and body shaming.[32] When asked by *Harper's Bazaar* magazine why SlutWalk is important right now, she explained:

> We have a voice and we all realize now that's why SlutWalk is so important...I think that whether being

---

32   Nadja Sayej, "'It's My Ass and My Instagram': Amber Rose Is Over Your Slut-Shaming," *Harper's Bazaar,* September 25, 2018.

sexually assaulted or slut shamed... we're just not taking it anymore. If anyone says anything about sexy pictures that I post, I can take it as they're mad at me for my confidence and that's really none of my business. I can't help how they feel.[33]

By being on the receiving end of unwarranted verbal abuse, Misty and Amber Rose know firsthand that the critique isn't about whatever they're wearing. The hate speech is really about these women being unapologetically confident about themselves and their bodies.

The audacity to be confident when you're considered by society as "too big, too small, too busty, too curvy, too skinny, too brown, or too pale," is an act of rebellion. Breaking free from those bounds is sexy, but it can be triggering to those still in bondage.

Pop star Lizzo is the best contemporary embodiment of this freedom. With a curvy plus-sized body that she has no problem baring and an eight-time Grammy-nominated album filled with self-affirming songs that will get you hyped enough to run a marathon or dump your boyfriend, Lizzo is a one-woman revolution.

British Vogue magazine explains that while there should technically be nothing revolutionary about a woman over a size fourteen singing about loving herself, this is the same reason so many women see themselves in Lizzo. In today's image-obsessed age, she is a megawatt beacon of

33   Ibid.

self-assurance—so utterly herself that it is impossible for it not to rub off on you.[34]

That's exactly her mission. "I'm not trying to sell you me," she proclaims. "I'm trying to sell you, *you.*" [35]

SEXY SELF-MASTERY

I now realize that my envy of Alexis isn't about the attention she gets from men, but it's about the attention she gives to herself. She can command a room because she's got complete control of who she is. Over another round of martinis, I discovered that Alexis wasn't born with this "sexy self-mastery." She had to earn it.

"The confidence I have now didn't come to me until after my divorce," she shared. "It was then that it was no longer about trying to live up to my ex-husband's expectations of how I should behave and dress. I had spent so many years trying to be someone else, but the divorce forced me to get to know my own personality and style. I finally stopped giving a damn about what everyone else thought about me and started living for myself."

After Alexis said that, I remember letting out a long, heavy sigh. Maybe it was the martinis, but I started to feel lighter, like a weight was coming off my chest. "There's still hope for me," I replied.

---

34 Zing Tsjeng, "Lizzo: 'I'm Not Trying to Sell You Me. I'm Trying to Sell You, You,'" *Vogue Britain,* November 9, 2019.

35 Ibid.

"Of course, there is!" Alexis exclaimed. "And now you know why so many women over forty become cougars and date younger men: our sexiness comes from knowing who we are, And we're no longer afraid to ask for what we want."

I think I've evolved into someone pretty confident - in myself and in my skin.

–HALLE BERRY

I've always been impatient. So instead of wasting four more years feeling awkward at the nightclub while waiting for the clock to strike midnight on my fortieth birthday, I've begun working on my "sexy self-mastery." Sticking to my spiritual practice, reading the books I enjoy, doing the work I'm meant to do, and laughing with my girlfriends all increase my self-confidence.

Slowly but surely, who I am is becoming a matter of fact, not focus. What I think about myself isn't dependent on attention (or lack thereof) from anyone.

Another Oprah-approved author, Glennon Doyle, describes perfectly the kind of "sex appeal" I desire:

> I think sexy is a grown-up word to describes a person who's confident that she is already exactly who she was made to be. A sexy woman knows herself and she likes the way she looks, thinks, & feels. She doesn't try to change to match anybody else... She doesn't hide her

true self because she is not ashamed. She knows she's just human—exactly how God made her, and that's good enough. Real sexy is letting your true self come out of hiding...[36]

Now I see what my father meant when he advised me to "just be myself" before every date. But as much as my love of sweatpants is a part of me, showing up in them for a first date probably isn't what Dad meant.

LEATHER PANTS AND POMPOMS

Whether it's a night out on the town with the girls, "sip and see" drinks with a guy from online, or a weekly date night with your high-school sweetheart, picking out the perfect outfit can be tricky. How do you show "what you're working with" without overdoing it? How can you show that you're comfortable in your own skin if you're not comfortable in that dress?

> There is definitely something sexy about a girl with an attitude and a pair of leather pants.
>
> —ELIZA DUSHKU

---

36   Glennon Doyle, *Love Warrior* (New York: Flatiron Books, 2017).

While not quite as comfortable as sweatpants, my pair of faux-leather leggings feel like "dressy sweatpants" and help me feel like a rock star. Paired with a tee shirt and blazer or a tunic sweater, I feel sexy but still covered.

While taking a pole-dancing class for a bachelorette party, it dawned on me why leather is so alluring. As I was struggling to climb the pole, the instructor yelled, "If you can't get on the pole, just stroke and caress your body! Touching yourself makes your audience want to touch you."

Fabrics like leather, suede, lace, and satin are deemed "sexy" because they evoke a desire to touch. Not only do those fabrics look sexy to the admirer but they feel good on the skin, making us, the wearer, feel sexy—hence why your "special occasion" panties probably aren't made of cotton.

Speaking of panties, I picked up a good tip about those from Kimberly, a former sergeant in the army. When you first meet Kimberly in her pearls and "conservatively covered" dresses, you'd compare her to a GI Jane version of Charlotte from "Sex in the City." But don't let that fool you, because there's definitely a Samantha hidden under those dresses.

"One night after work, I met my husband at an event for his company," she fondly recalled. "When I walked into the ballroom, I whispered in his ear, 'I'm not wearing any underwear.' Despite me having on this basic black 'work dress,' he couldn't stop staring at me the entire night. I've never felt sexier."

While Kimberly's alluring moment came from an intentional decision, sometimes it's our unintentional ones that drive someone wild. Years ago, I remember my older cousin Eric telling me how he met his girlfriend on the first day of his freshman year at college. "She was walking to class that morning," he said with a smile. "I don't remember what she was wearing but I do remember she had on a pair of running shoes and ankle socks that had little pompoms on them. I don't know what it was about those socks and sneakers, but I chased her down and asked for her phone number." They've been together ever since.

Leather or lace. Lingerie or nothing. High heels or sneakers. Socks or no socks. There's no such thing as "sexy clothes." Whatever makes you feel like the most confident version of yourself is sexy.

No matter your bra size or your hair color, you're already perfectly gorgeous. You just have to own it. And when the attention comes, instead of running, revel in being admired. You're worthy because you are a sight to behold.

WORTHY WRAP-UP

1. Never downplay your sex appeal. Sexiness does not come from your body shape, your weight, your age, your hair color, or your makeup. Work with what you've got while staying within the boundaries of what's appropriate for the occasion.
2. Enhance yourself with makeup, hair, and clothes to be the best version of you, not to look like a substandard copy of someone else.

3. What someone else thinks about you is none of your business. And your opinions of another woman say more about you than her.
4. Have fun with sensual fabrics and styles. Try a leather dress or a lace blouse or red pumps.
5. Confidence is the sexiest thing you can ever put on.

WORTHY WORDS

I am sexy and safe.

PART THREE

PLENTY

CHAPTER 9

LET GO

I once lost a tug-of-war battle with a seventy-one-year-old woman. It was a literal knock-down, drag-out fight, with Mrs. Rose knocking me down and dragging me across the carpet of her closet as I held onto her biscuit-beige, pearl-buttoned, wide-lapel Kasper pantsuit for dear life.

Refusing to be defeated by her and the suit, I yelled, "LET IT GO!"

Refusing to be bossed around, Mrs. Rose countered with an aggressive, "I WILL NOT!"

When I first started my business, two girlfriends hired me to help their recently retired mom get a clean closet and a fresh look for this next phase in her life. Excited to get my first "out-of-town client," I traveled to St. Louis, presumably to help "a sweet old lady find clothes for her new life of leisure." Instead, I was greeted by a tall, no-nonsense woman who, like her namesake, was beautiful but thorny.

After working forty-four years as a middle school administrator, Mrs. Rose was used to being in charge. She had four closets worth of suits that signaled that same level of authority. Pantsuits, skirt suits, lavender suits, pistachio green suits, tweed suits, linen suits, seersucker suits—each with matching blouse, jewelry, and shoes. All with one singular message: "Preteen, do not even try me. I am in charge."

Yet I, who was no longer a preteen and, in fact, was a grown-ass woman, still fell victim to the power of the suit, per the carpet burn on my backside.

Looking back, our tug-of-war shouldn't have been a total surprise. The first two hours and two closets were a bit arduous, with Mrs. Rose longingly touching each suit and fabricating ways she could wear it to her charity functions and volunteer events or promising that her mother could use the suit for church. Naive and still wet behind the ears as a stylist, I (somewhat) believed her—until there were more suits still hanging in the closets than in the donation bag.

By the time we reached the basement closet, I had found my gumption and exerted my expertise on said Beige Bomber.

"Mrs. Rose, seriously, this suit has to be older than I am," I said while mockingly holding it up in front of me. "When was the last time you wore it?'"

"Just because it's old, Morgan, doesn't mean it's out of style."

"While in some cases that may be true, Mrs. Rose, that logic does not apply here. And you didn't answer my question. It's got to go."

Before the suit even left my hand, Mrs. Rose desperately grabbed it, almost yanking my arm from its socket. The war was on. While there's a very good chance Mrs. Rose had more muscle than me, what truly made her victorious in the "Battle of the Beige" was her refusal to let go of the past.

After Mrs. Rose and I both caught our breath, I asked her what was really so special about that suit. "It's not about that specific suit," she confided, "but about seeing forty-four years of my life get tossed into trash bags. I wore these suits every day. They became part of my identity. And now that I'm no longer a principal, I don't quite know who I am."

ATTACHMENT OR FEAR

Everyone's favorite tidy-upper, Marie Kondo, put to words what Mrs. Rose was experiencing in her closet: "When we really delve into the reasons for why we can't let something go, there are only two—an attachment to the past or a fear for the future."

In the case of Mrs. Rose and many other women, it might be a mix of both. Either way, it's the inability to accept and honor the present. When it comes to having great style, accepting who you are is critical—not who you *were* five years ago, fifteen pounds ago, three jobs ago, or two kids ago, but who you are *right now.*

> *By curating a closet for the woman you are today; you're not forgetting the past or erasing the memories (that's what Facebook is for). Instead, you're honoring how those past experiences helped you become the woman you are now.*

While a life transition as major as Mrs. Rose's can certainly be terrifying, holding on to those suits wouldn't make it less scary. Those suits weren't really a security blanket. They were dead weight holding her back from fully entering this next phase.

During a Sunday sermon at my beloved church, Hillside International Truth Center, Bishop Jack Bomar compelled us to "take our grave clothes off and start living life to the fullest." While some may read John 11:44 and think of "grave clothes" solely as the clothes in which we are buried, in the context of the sermon and this book, our grave clothes are the things keeping us stuck in the past.

For some women like Mrs. Rose, their grave clothes reflect an inability to accept a change in profession and a shift in purpose. For other women, their closet grief is about their bodies.

As we age, life happens. Our bodies evolve. Some things become bigger; others smaller. Accepting those changes isn't always easy, but acceptance of the present is the only way.

Sometimes you have to be willing to let go of something old to grab onto something new. You have to be willing to let a part of you die that you used to be comfortable with in order for another part of you to be born.

– LISA NICHOLS

While in the closet of an uber-successful real estate agent, I uncovered that the real reason Abby didn't enjoy getting dressed each morning was that she was forced to face an entire size four wardrobe that no longer fit. Those grave clothes were a constant reminder of what size she *used* to wear, the life she *used* to live, and the person she *used* to be.

Instead of celebrating the beautifully curvy body, amazing kids, and successful life she had now, Abby was mourning the loss of her old self. Her drab wardrobe reflected that. It was time for us to remove her grave clothes from the closet so that each morning, she could be confident and excited about the life she's living right now.

BECOMING THE WOMAN YOU WANT TO BE

According to *Forbes*, the average American consumer owns 120 pieces of clothing but only wears 20 percent of what they own.[37] That's twenty-four items you're probably wearing over and over again. That remaining 80 percent is purely dead weight taking up space.

While the idea of only owning the twenty-four items terrifies me, my good friend, Shannon, is a courageous over-achiever, getting her entire closet down to nineteen items. *Nineteen.*

- Three tee shirts (two black and one grey)
- Denim shirt
- Black turtleneck
- Black jeans
- Black skirt
- Black dress
- White dress
- Cutoff denim shorts
- Black pumps
- Black booties
- Two pairs of sandals
- Two pairs of sneakers
- Camel wool coat

---

37   Deborah Weinswig, "Millennials Go Minimal: The Decluttering Lifestyle Trend That Is Taking Over," *Forbes*.

- Black leather jacket
- Black puffer coat

Shannon doesn't have so few items just because she likes extra space in her closet. It's about her finally becoming the woman she's always wanted to be. After closing her restaurant in favor of traveling and writing, she was also ready to shed the excess clothes that no longer served her.

Shannon explained to me what prompted her closet catharsis: "With so many changes happening, I started becoming incredibly intentional about the life I wanted to create for myself. The kind of work I do, the people I interact with, the experiences I want to have, and my style. Now I'm constantly assessing and editing." With a quiet sense of determination, she continued, "If something or someone or an opportunity is in alignment with my goals, then it stays. If it isn't, it goes."

The more you know, the less you need.

– ABORIGINAL SAYING

And while a tightly curated, minimalist capsule wardrobe would be absolute torture for me, Shannon is like a butterfly escaping from the cocoon of an overstuffed closet. She's also never looked better. With a fresh short pixie haircut that mirrors her minimal wardrobe, her image is the perfect match for her new lifestyle and values.

"But don't you ever miss having options?" I asked.

"Not at all," Shannon countered. "Getting dressed each morning is so much easier. As a matter of fact, years ago, I created a Pinterest board with my ideal style. Now I finally have it. While this will sound crazy to you, my nineteen items are truly my dream wardrobe."

YOUR SACRED SPACE

When it comes to building a worthy wardrobe, there is a happy medium between Shannon's nineteen items and Mrs. Rose's four closets. Whatever your magic number of items is, your closet should be your happy place. Let it be the place that gets you excited for the day ahead, boosting your confidence and honoring the beautiful woman you are.

Before we start assessing and editing the clothes in your closet, take this as a friendly reminder that your closet is not a catch-all for junk: not your kids' trophies, your old tax returns, or your husband's fishing poles. Honor that special place with *only* the things that bring you joy.

Your closet is your sacred space for you to enjoy preparing to face the day. I know when Jesus said to go into your closet to pray, he wasn't talking about your literal closet, but the idea holds true. A clean closet helps you start the day clear-headed. Instead of being anxious and frustrated after digging through piles of decades-old debris, you'll start your morning centered and at peace.

To make your closet a sacred place that you enjoy opening the doors to, try some of these ideas:

- Create a "vision board" by taping photos and magazine clippings of words and images that inspire you to your closet door.
- Invest in a pretty, full length mirror.
- Replace the wire hangers from the dry cleaners with velvet or wooden ones.
- Display your jewelry on stands (you can find these online or at an organizational store) or install a sculptural piece of art on your walls that has "branches" for you to hang necklaces and scarves.
- Show off your shoes and handbags by taking them out of their boxes. You won't wear what you can't see.
- Use file dividers from the office supply store to organize your clutches.
- Cubby shelves work for folded jeans and sweaters.
- Light the room up with fancy (or Christmas) lights.
- Add a soft fuzzy rug and a bench to put on your shoes.
- Decorate with delectable candles and flowers.

These little touches help make the act of getting dressed a ritual. The beautiful woman that you are deserves it.

HAVE FAITH

"But I might need that later!"

It never fails that I will hear that whine at least once while cleaning out a closet. And my response is always, "Have faith and trust God enough to know that the next time you need a pair of low-rise jeans with rhinestones on the pocket, you'll have the means to acquire them."

While there's a clinical diagnosis for extreme hoarding, in my line of work, I consider a client who is unwilling to let things go as someone who has forgotten (or maybe never even realized) that God *always* provides. If you've acquired new clothes once, you can do it again.

Holding on to things that no longer serve you sends a message to God that you don't trust Her enough to take care of all your needs. And as powerful divine beings, our subconscious mind is eager to prove our logic right, quickly creating experiences of lack.

Our experiences, surroundings, and closets are external expressions of our inner subconscious thoughts. By clearing your closet, you now have the physical and emotional space to shop for clothes that reflect your worthiness.

According to her Facebook page, Mrs. Rose is currently living her best retired life. She's been so busy traveling to Italy, volunteering with her church, and co-chairing charitable causes that she doesn't have time to even think about that biscuit-beige suit she fought me for.

WORTHY WRAP-UP

1. Release the attachment to the past and the predictions of the future. Shed your grave clothes and honor the amazing woman you are right now.
2. Edit out what's merely taking up space and only keep the items that are in alignment with you.
3. Your closet is meant to be a place that gets you excited about getting dressed each morning. Don't settle for anything less.
4. Have faith that you will always have what you need when you need it.
5. Let go of the past and start living your absolute best life.

WORTHY WORDS

I release all that no longer serves me, and I open myself up to new possibilities.

CHAPTER 10

CLEANING OUT
THE CLOSET

———

Because curating a closet is about honoring that woman in the mirror, we must get clear on who that woman is. That means pulling out the literal and figurative skeletons in your closet. Things may get messy and even a bit emotional, but there's always a breakthrough after the breakdown.

Before you get overwhelmed with determining what stays and what goes, here are some truths I affirm whenever I clean out a closet (even my own).

#1 REMEMBER THAT YOU ARE DIVINE

You might have spent some years covered up in mud and frumpy cardigans, but you are still a Golden Buddha. Forgive yourself for your past life and wardrobe mistakes. We all have them. Don't get stuck there.

Before going through your closet, stand in front of the mirror and state the affirmation *"I am perfect just as I am"* repeatedly until you start to believe it. Then turn on some Lizzo, Chaka Kahn, or Taylor Swift, dance around, and decide today that you're worthy of clothes that make you feel and look amazing.

Let go of anything that doesn't make you feel like you belong on a stage belting out "Shake It Off."

Happiness and confidence are the prettiest things you can wear.

— TAYLOR SWIFT

#2 ACCEPT YOUR SIZE

When determining if an item stays or goes, the first qualifier is whether or not it fits. Not "used to fit," not "might fit if I don't eat, breathe, walk, or sit down," but fits and feels comfortable *right now*. And beyond just fitting—the garment must *flatter* you. There's a difference.

Something that fits you means it works for your weight and height (your approximate size). Something that flatters you means that it enhances your shape. One of the many amazing things about clothes is that they are our personal magicians—instantly creating the illusion of more of this or less of that. When you know your body shape and have come to peace with your current size, the right cut of pants will make you look longer and leaner.

If you try something on and your eyes go immediately to your least favorite parts of your body, then repeat step one of affirming your perfection and then toss that thing in the donation bag.

The feng shui definition of clutter is "postponed decisions and the inability to move forward."[38] Clutter holds us back and keeps us from making progress. If you're like Abby, who was holding on to the too-small pre-babies clothes, I beg you to please let the "One Days" go.

The "One Day" you lose the baby weight and can fit into those jeans from college may never come. In the meantime, you'll beat yourself up every morning, being held captive to the mythical place of "One Day" instead of being excited about today.

Even if you're on a major fitness and lifestyle change, I guarantee that the woman you will become after losing the weight will want clothes that glorify and respect this new evolution, not old jeans from freshman year. Just because you can fit them doesn't mean you *should* wear them. A drastic change

---

38   John Rozenberg, "Clearing Clutter – Beyond the Closet," Spirit Walk (blog), December 2, 2015.

in size is a great opportunity to update your image and start exploring new options that honor the new woman you are.

Once the weight you work to lose does come off, I also implore you to immediately let go of the items that are now too big. Or take them to a tailor to get them taken in. As someone whose weight has fluctuated drastically, I used to keep my larger-sized jeans "just in case." But then I realized I was sending a signal to the universe that I wanted to wear them again, so my subconscious mind got to work helping me fulfill that request—thanks to binges of cookies and PB&Js. Of course, keeping things within a one-size range makes sense as our weight naturally fluctuates, but anything bigger or smaller than one size has got to go.

#3 BE HONEST ABOUT YOUR LIFESTYLE

Now that Mrs. Rose wasn't going into the trenches of middle school, she no longer needed her suited armor. Her life now consisted of travel, country clubs, volunteering, and fundraising, requiring more refined elegance than authority. While we got rid of the traditional business formal suits, we kept her chic and comfy St. John's knit suits. Instead of wearing them as suits, we paired the stretchy and colorful jackets with jeans, and the pants and skirts with tee shirts and jean jackets. We donated the modest pumps and replaced them with spunky new sneakers and fancy flat sandals. And with the old suits gone, we created more space for the new gowns she needs for her high society formals.

At my last corporate job, I existed almost entirely in the land of business casual, wearing jeans, pointed-toe flats, a cashmere sweater, and a fancy necklace to work every day. I had an insane number of jeans and an even crazier number of flats. I'm *nobody's* minimalist. For the occasional night out on the town, I had a few pairs of Satan Stilettos that would require me to find a chair the minute we walked (or, in my case, hobbled) into the bar.

Thanks to entrepreneurship, my networking and speaking engagements require more business formal attire than ever before. As hard as it was to let them go, I'm now down to four pairs of jeans (which is still quadruple what Shannon owns). While I don't have a clue how many items I own, my current closet consists of 75 percent dresses, pleated skirts, and a few pairs of slacks and blouses. The few tee shirts and sweaters I own are now nestled into a few cubby holes.

Sometimes you've got to let everything go— purge yourself. If you are unhappy with anything ... whatever is bringing you down, get rid of it. Because you'll find that when you're free, your true creativity, your true self comes out.

−TINA TURNER

As for shoes, I'd love to be the kind of woman who can spend all day in four-inch stilettos. But I am not. I am a woman with the gait of a tyrannosaurus rex. So to avoid drawing even more attention to my aggressive stride, I purged the shoes I couldn't walk in, keeping only the modest two to three-inch heels I could handle. I also got rid of most of my flats, as the days when I'm on my feet the longest are the days I'm shopping with a client, and sneakers are the most comfortable option.

But here's the thing, just because you *think* your life doesn't require much more than business casual, that doesn't give you permission to be boring or bland. Don't be like I was during my cubicle days—wearing nothing but jeans and solid sweaters. Instead, go into your sacred space and have some fun.

Challenge yourself to play in your closet and create new outfits with what you already own:

1. Pull out a blouse, walk slowly through your closet with the blouse held in front of you.
2. Find three different bottoms you haven't worn with the blouse before. Try mixing patterns (for example, stripes and florals are amazing together) or do red pants instead of basic black.
3. Complete each pairing with a "third piece": a necklace, blazer, cardigan, or statement shoe that turns a blouse and a bottom into an "outfit."
4. Take pictures of yourself in each new outfit and wear one new look a week.

While purging, make sure you're still prepared for life's other occasions. Keep a few business formal pieces, like a skirt or pantsuit, just in case your dream job calls. And make sure to have a cocktail dress, heels, and clutch ready for a last-minute invite.

Just like with dating, nothing is worse than being desperate when you're shopping. You settle for the first thing you find, even if you don't really like the guy or the dress. By keeping a few special pieces in your closet, you can spend the day of an event relaxing or preparing your answer for the inevitable "tell me about a time when..." interview question instead of scrambling for an outfit at the mall. Even Shannon has a little black dress for when she needs to close the deal on a business venture or a guy.

#4 DETERMINE YOUR GOALS AND MOTIVATIONS

In my workshops and with my clients, the first question I ask is, "What do you want to be known for?" Because this question can be a bit challenging to answer, I give my signature style assessment that combines personality traits with personal and professional goals.

Some people call this "building your personal brand," but I would challenge that "building a brand" feels a bit contrived and inauthentic. This is more about giving yourself permission to show the world your personality and your purpose. Once the client and I get clear on what she's trying to accomplish, we can then easily determine if a garment, shoe, or accessory supports those goals.

When a woman is living in her truth,
she is radiant in whatever she's wearing.

Denise is the coolest HR executive I've ever met and a perfect example of said radiance. I meet many HR ladies in my work, but never had I met one who moonlights as the lead singer for a punk rock band. After she hired me to give a keynote at the medical device factory she led in conservative Gainesville, Florida, I inquired about her rock star swag in a sea of Lily Pulitzer paisley. Denise explained:

> HR in general is known as the standard setter. We write the "rules" and are supposed to represent the company's values. I use my wardrobe to give our engineers the message and unspoken permission that it's okay to be themselves here. I want to make them feel comfortable in my presence so that they trust me.
>
> I also want to be an example of how they can bring more of their personality to the workplace. While I'm always professional and appropriate, I make sure to make a statement. Sometimes it's gigantic funky earrings, other times it's a blouse with lightning rods printed all over it. This is also about me breaking the mold of what it means to be a middle-aged woman and an HR executive. I want to show people they can do anything, even start a punk rock band when you're thirty-five.

Once Denise got clear about her goals and message and what she wanted the world to know about her, she got rid of any outliers. Because her wardrobe is now consistent with who she is, getting dressed each morning is a breeze and her "personal brand" comes naturally.

Several times, I've walked into a woman's closet and it looks like five different women live there. There's the bohemian printed blouses and fringe bags; the traditional preppy tweed blazers and gingham check shirts; the sexy sky-high stilettos and bright red body-con dresses. While nothing is wrong with being versatile, not having a clear style identity makes it hard to create a consistent personal style. Items from one style profile often don't mix with others, causing chaos when trying to create an outfit each morning.

You can't be hesitant about who you are.

–VIOLA DAVIS

A scatter-brained closet also hints at insecurity in not being totally aware of who you are and what you have to offer.

Here's an activity to streamline your style:

1. Divide your clothes into "personality piles":

    a. The "Minimalist": sleek, solid pieces with clean sharp lines
    b. The "Rockstar": edgy, leather, studded and textured items
    c. The "Romantic": sweet, pastel, ruffled, pleated styles with lace or intricate details
    d. The "Creative": funky, printed, artistic, vintage finds
    e. The "Classic": conservative "preppy" aesthetic with pearls, nautical stripes, and traditional silhouettes

f. The "Sporty": casual, athletic, and outdoorsy-inspired plaids and fabrics.

2. Take an honest look at each pile. It's perfectly normal to be a mix of style intuitions, but anything more than two large piles gets complicated. It's also to be expected that as you grow and evolve, so will your style.

   Which one feels the most like you right now and represents the message you're trying to send? Prioritize that as your primary "style intuition." Let's say vintage jackets and bell-bottoms worked for the bohemian lifestyle of your early twenties. Now that you're a marketing executive, you may lean more toward "Rockstar."

3. Go through the secondary piles and keep only the items that work with the items in the primary pile. For example, if a classic traditional Jackie O. look is how you want to show up, then keep your timeless shift dresses and peep-toe pumps. For more casual occasions, wear your leather jacket from the Rockstar pile instead of a navy blazer. Get rid of the flowy printed maxi dresses that don't feel like you.

The Grand Dame Oprah Winfrey advises, "As you become more clear about who you really are, you can better decide what is best for you—the first time around." The more you practice wearing what feels true to you, the easier wardrobe creation becomes.

#5 GET IN TOUCH WITH YOUR PREFERENCES

By holding true to your own sense of style, you'll free your-self from the wardrobe tastes, preferences, and choices of anyone else. If I had a nickel for every time a woman told me, "Oh, I can't get rid of that sweater/dress/necklace because my mother/sister/husband/friend gave it to me," I'd be a mil-lionaire already.

When I ask, "But do *you* like it?" the response is almost always the deafening sound of silence.

Many women are so used to dressing up (or down) to the expectations of others that they don't even know what they like anymore. They're almost like the princess-to-be in my favorite movie, *Coming to America*. When Imani (Vanessa Bell Calloway) first meets Prince Akeem (Eddie Murphy), she proudly tells him that her entire life has been focused on being groomed to become his bride and that she likes "what-ever he likes." But wanting to get to know the woman he's supposed to spend his entire life with, he says in exasperation, "I know what I like. And I know you know what I like. But I want to know what *you* like." Imani couldn't answer him and was promptly shown the door.

While many women have been taught that being accom-modating is a virtue, not speaking up about what you want makes it impossible to have a personal style. Prince Akeem's eye rolls and eventual dismissal of the Eager Pleaser proves this habit is also frustrating to everyone else.

By keeping and wearing unloved gifted items, we're holding ourselves hostage to the idea of who our loved ones want us to be, expect us to be, or are used to us being. It stunts our evolution and clutters our closets.

It's okay to tell your sister you don't want her hand-me-downs, or to get store credit for the scarf your mother bought you for Christmas. They love you, and their intention behind the gift was wanting you to enjoy it.

True love is about wanting the other person to get what they want, not wanting them to wear your gift simply out of "obligation." And besides, it's much easier to say on Christmas morning, "I love you and appreciate your thoughtfulness. This isn't quite my style. How about we go shopping together?" than having to lie later when they ask, "Why haven't you worn that purple polka-dotted skirt I got you?"

Honesty with yourself and your loved ones is always the best policy.

Even if you did hit the jackpot with "great gift-giving relatives," deciding whether an item stays or goes isn't just about whether you love the item (or the person who gave it to you). Even though that dress might "spark joy"[39] for you, it must also fit your body, your lifestyle, and your message. Otherwise, let it go.

---

39   Marie Kondo, *Spark Joy: An Illustrated Master Class on the Art of Organizing and Tidying Up* (New York: Random House, 2015).

LET GO AND LET GOD

If any of those five truths were hard for you to handle, don't beat yourself up. Cleaning out our closet can be very emotional, bringing up memories we had "packed away," feelings we don't want to feel, and questions for which we don't have immediate answers.

Instead of avoiding the process, surrender it all to God. A simple prayer like, *"Show me who I'm meant to be and help me become her"* will get you answers if you pay attention. Little clues will start appearing. Conversations with strangers will confirm your ideas. Opportunity will knock at your door.

> Growing up, I didn't know what I wanted to do, but I knew the kind of woman I wanted to be.
>
> —DIANE VON FURSTENBERG

As you evolve into the woman you want to be, remember: your worthiness comes from the divine power within you, not from clothes that no longer serve you. Whatever you're struggling to let go of, such as the business suits from a former job, or clothes that no longer fit, or unwanted gifts from family members, let those items be a blessing to someone else. Letting go becomes easier by finding a place to donate your items, leaving you with a good feeling about where they went.

After going through your closets, quickly get the unwanted items out of your house. The longer they stay, the less likely you'll be able to let them go for good. Several thrift stores and charities provide free pick-up services. Check if a local homeless shelter or church is in need of clothing donations. You can even find more specific organizations looking for certain types of clothing.

For example, by letting go of the business attire you no longer need, someone else can wear it to an interview or to work via an organization that will pair your clothing with the right person in need. Dress for Success is my favorite non-profit to donate business formal and business casual items from my own closet and the closets of my clients. Dress for Success' nationwide chapters are committed to helping women in challenging life circumstances get a fresh start, offering job-readiness training, and providing participants clothes to help them ace their new job opportunities. Many colleges can also use your gently used, work-ready attire for students unable to afford new suits. Let those long-unused suits be a blessing to another woman in need.

By opening ourselves and our closets to God, we can make peace with the past and focus on the only thing that matters—the present. By releasing the pressures and predictions of the "One Days," we are exercising our faith that God's plans are always bigger than the ones we have for ourselves. And once we get out of God's way, She can do Her best work, surprising us beyond our wildest dreams.

WORTHY WRAP-UP

1. Decide today that you're worthy of clothes that make you feel and look amazing.
2. If it doesn't fit *and* flatter your current size and shape, it's got to go.
3. Give yourself permission to show the world your personality and your purpose through your clothes.
4. Honesty with yourself, your loved ones, and the Universe is always the best policy.
5. Let go of the past and let God amaze you beyond your wildest dreams.

WORTHY WORDS

My closet is the perfect reflection of the woman I am.

CHAPTER 11

STOP SETTLING

I've never had to ask a client where she keeps her clothes, but there's a first time for everything.

Hannah found me through the internet. When we had our first consult call, she told me she had recently been laid off and was back on the job market. Because of her uncertain job status, she was a little hesitant about investing in my services and a new wardrobe. The more she talked, the more I could tell she wasn't just unsure about her job status. She was also unsure about herself. I told her that while I totally understood her financial situation, a new wardrobe might be what she needs to boost her confidence while she interviews. I sent her some interview tips and told her to get back to me when she made her decision.

After a few days, Hannah decided to move forward, and I went to her home for her first session. In the first few seconds in her home, I knew our work together was about more than just new interview clothes. As she gave me a tour of the house, I noticed the master bedroom and closet were overflowing with her husband's clothes and sneakers. Nike boxes were stacked everywhere—in the closet shelves, lining the bedroom walls, under the bed. Everywhere I turned, there was a sneaker. "My husband is a basketball coach, so sneakers are an obsession of his," Hannah revealed. "My son is the same way too."

"So where are your clothes?" I asked.

As we walked down the hall, Hannah said, "I share a closet with my daughter in her room."

In the small closet in her nine-year-old daughter's room, Hannah's clothes were hanging, and her daughter's clothes were folded in cubbies at the bottom (and strewn about on the floor). Compared to everyone else in the family, Hannah's clothes were by far the oldest and the cheapest: outdated blazers from Target's junior department; yellowing white slacks; and boxy, shapeless church dresses her mother had passed down to her.

As I did my initial assessment, I asked, "When's the last time you went shopping for yourself?"

Hannah confirmed what I already knew: "It's probably been years."

Caught up in taking care of everyone else, Hannah had put herself at the bottom of the list. There were basketball games to attend, cheerleading squads to support, lunches to make, and errands to run.

The location of Hannah's clothes and the clothes themselves reflected that everyone else was more important than Hannah. This sense of unworthiness showed up not just in her clothes, but also through her wavering voice and struggles with making decisions.

> It is so liberating to really know what I want, what truly makes me happy, what I will not tolerate. I have learned that it is no one else's job to take care of me but me.
>
> —BEYONCÉ

The notion of spending thousands of dollars on herself and a new wardrobe was huge for Hannah. Our shopping trip was a step in changing how she treated herself and redefining her place in her family. Thanks to some great sales and coupons, I found Hannah a whole new wardrobe and shoe collection for under two thousand dollars, which was probably half the cost of her husband's sneaker collection. Outfitted with floral blazers, fitted dresses, leather leggings, high-waisted jeans, quality blouses, snakeskin pumps, and funky ankle booties, Hannah was prepared for any corporate dress code as well as for Saturdays spent as a sports mom.

SELF-RESPECT LOOKS GOOD ON YOU

In the days following our shopping session, I got pictures of Hannah rocking the blue and yellow floral blouse we purchased and a pair of black skinny jeans. She also sent me links of high heels she was considering purchasing. After congratulating her on her incredible progress, she replied:

> You have no idea how much of a struggle this is for me. I wake up at 3:00 a.m. sometimes worried that I have too many clothes. I contemplate sending back every order. I mentally calculate how many other things I could have bought for my kids for the price of a pair of shoes.
>
> Conversely, I get excited about putting together an outfit. I walk taller and look people in the eye a bit longer. I have finally started the small group for teenage girls that I've been wanting to do, and I started working in the production team at church after three years of dismissing my passion. I love that people ask me where I got my clothes. I like how self-respect feels.

My heart broke a little but also beamed with pride. If you relate to Hannah's struggle, then my response to her is also for you:

> Thank you for sharing with me and allowing me to join you in this process. You're truly going through a transformation, and I'm so excited for you. But here's the deal—until you truly believe and KNOW that you're just as worthy of new clothes as your husband and kids are, you'll be second-guessing every single purchase.

Seeing yourself in new clothes that reflect how beautiful you are will help, but self-love is an everyday job that everyone is working on.

And just remember, how you treat yourself is the example you're giving your daughter about how she should think about herself and your son an example of how women should be valued.

Over the course of the year since those first sessions, I've witnessed Hannah's evolution—a cute short haircut that makes a statement and bold jewelry that announces her presence. She didn't get the job I initially helped prepare her for, but she gained so much more.

I even returned to Hannah's home for another interview prep session. The changes in her were impossible to ignore. Her glow and pride were infectious. While her new clothes were still in her daughter's room, some of her husband's sneaker boxes in the master bedroom had been replaced with high heels.

During that session, we decided she would wear cobalt blue slacks and a black and white striped blouse topped with a black blazer to this next interview. Her boldness and confidence helped her ace the interview and land her dream job.

You teach people how to treat you, and one of the ways people learn how is by observing how you treat yourself. That includes your image. By making the investment in herself,

Hannah was sending a message to her family and future coworkers that they, too, must invest in her.

LEVEL UP

For some of us, our mental blocks when it comes to shopping isn't about actually shopping but about the price. After spending almost every weekend of my childhood in T.J. Maxx, I am obsessed with finding a bargain. Working in retail and learning how little most items cost to make further fuels my determination not to pay full price for anything. I'm proud to pass on to my clients my skills in finding a great deal.

But there's a difference between scoring big at a sale and settling. While interviewing Joanne, she told me how a blazer helped her realize she had been doing the latter. Like me, Joanne had lived her whole life with her wardrobe being totally dependent on what was on the clearance rack. Even if the pants were a little short or she didn't exactly love the color of the blouse, she bought them because they were the least expensive option.

A few years ago, that mindset shifted while preparing to interview for a job significantly higher than her current level and pay grade. When shopping for what to wear on the big day, she found a grey blazer that fit her perfectly and gave her the professional look she wanted. Priced at seventy dollars, it was higher than she was used to paying for a single item. But something shifted for her in that store. "While looking at myself in the fitting room mirror, I realized that if I wanted to level up in my career, I had to level up in my wardrobe," Joanne recalled. "Even though the idea of paying the full price of seventy dollars killed me, I did it. I love that blazer and wore it long after getting that job."

> I always believed that when you follow your heart or your gut, when you really follow the things that feel great to you, you can never lose, because settling is the worst feeling in the world.
>
> —RIHANNA

Joanne's story is a great example of how many of us are conditioned to only like something if it's on sale. That's why many stores inflate their original ticket prices, often called the Manufacturer's Suggested Retail Price (MSRP). That way, when they do offer a sale (often right as the product hits the store or online), you get the impression you're getting a deal when it's actually the price the store planned to sell it at all along.

Another example is using 0.99 cent endings to make you think the item costs less than it actually does, or an even number like one hundred dollars to give the item an air of prestige. As a merchant, it was my job to get good at this game. At the start of each season, I created a plan for how many weeks (or days) a garment would be full price, then 25 percent off, and then back to full price, and then down to 50 percent off before a final price of clearance, which meant it got a 0.99 cent ending to imply "bargain" and get all the remaining inventory out the door quickly.

These tricks are called "psychological pricing" because they're obviously used to appeal to our psyche, but there's a deeper element to our beliefs around pricing. The habit of only shopping the clearance rack is rooted in not believing we're worthy enough to pay full price. Before Joanne bought that blazer, she always settled for things simply because they were on sale. This created closet items that didn't excite her, didn't work well together, and just made her feel "'ho-hum" when she put them on.

Joanne, and you, are worthy of more. Worthy of better. Worthy of clothes you enjoy wearing that make you proud of the message they send. This isn't about breaking the bank and buying things you can't afford. It's about adjusting your mindset to know that you deserve what you desire.

STEPPING OUT ON FAITH

One of my favorite authors is Paulo Coelho, the best-selling Brazilian author of all time. His world-famous book, *The Alchemist*, tells the story of a young boy on a mission to discover worldly treasures, only to discover that the true treasure he's been looking for is within. One of my favorite quotes from the book is framed on my bedroom wall: "When you want something, all the universe conspires in helping you to achieve it."[40]

---

40 Paulo Coelho, *The Alchemist* (New York: Harper Collins, 1993), 22.

When "Uncle" Paulo wrote these inspiring words, I guarantee he wasn't talking about shopping, but because it's true in all areas of life, I know this applies to wardrobe building as well. Take the case of my best friend, Lauren.

In 2011, both Lauren and I were living in New York City, enjoying the Big Apple as only twenty-somethings could. Despite both of us living paycheck to paycheck, we always miraculously met our needs for rent, happy hour, and unlimited mimosas. So imagine the shock when Lauren was laid off.

Of course, Lauren was worried about making ends meet, but she was also embarrassed. This wasn't supposed to happen to someone who was the first to arrive and last to leave every night. So much of Lauren's identity was connected to being a high-performing worker. *What would people think about her?*

When she finally got the nerve to share the news with some of her other girlfriends, Antoinette spoke faith and inspiration over her. "Girl, I'm not even worried about you. Trust and believe that you're never going to be in lack. You will always be in abundance. I even bet that you're going to end up with *two* checks." With her severance to run out in a few weeks and uncertainty about unemployment being able to cover rent, the idea of abundance was hard for Lauren to fathom. But thank God for friends whose belief is stronger than your unbelief.

A few weeks later, Antoinette's prophecy became a reality. The day after an interview for a job in media sales, Lauren got two checks in the mail—one from her old employer and one from unemployment, bigger than she had expected. With her monthly expenses being covered with the first check,

Lauren decided to use that second check to fulfill a long-standing desire.

Lauren later recalled, "I'd always wanted a Louis Vuitton tote bag. They have always been a symbol of success to me. But, of course, living on a New York City budget, I had never had the extra income to get one. As irresponsible as I know this sounds, I decided to use my extra check to get myself that bag. I saw myself walking into my new office, carrying that bag with my company-issued laptop inside."

I'll never forget the day Lauren got her dream bag. We met at the "Big Macy's" in Herald Square and anxiously went to the Louis Vuitton counter. Lauren tried the "opening price point" tote (a cool $1400) but fell in love with a bag that had more structure and a zippered compartment, perfect for holding a laptop. Including tax, the bag was over $1800, which was more than Lauren's rent, and more than she had expected to spend.

But instead of settling for what she didn't love, Lauren followed her heart. We were so nervous when she handed over her debit card, but we both knew she was making the right choice. I remember being so proud of Lauren for stepping out in faith and excited that "we" had our first LV!

I'd rather regret the risks that didn't work out than the chances I didn't take at all.

−SIMONE BILES

Two days later, Lauren got the job. And a week later, she carried that LV into the office, feeling like the Boss she is.

This purchase was significant because it was an application of Lauren's trust and faith that she would be okay. It was *not* because it was a designer bag. Actually, it wasn't even about the bag itself. This distinction is important because countless women identify their worth by the number of designer labels they wear.

Investing in items that fit and honor you and your budget is style. Wearing something just because it's a "status symbol" is insecurity.

As counterintuitive as it sounds, "over-done designer" is like a layer of mud, covering up your Golden Buddha. Instead of seeing who you are, the world only sees someone else's brand. There's nothing wrong with desiring well-made, high-quality designer pieces and investing in your image. My next big "made it" purchase will probably be a quilted Chanel bag that I'll pass down to my future daughter.

But there's a difference between appreciation and dependence. You don't need someone's else name on your chest to validate who you are. You're worthy of being seen as *you,* not as a billboard.

Lauren's new bag was about silencing the nagging thoughts in her head that she wasn't a success because she'd been laid off. That LV, which she still carries to this day; ten years later, represents an investment she made in an item she loves because she knows she's worthy of it, no matter her job title. It also serves as a visual reminder that God not only provides for our needs but also our desires.

When you get serious about what you want, God gets serious with you, conspiring to make your desires a reality.

This promise is summed up in Jesus' statement, "Do not be afraid, little flock, for your Father is pleased to give you the kingdom."[41] As children of God, we are not meant to live in poverty. It's our God-given right to live an abundant life right here and right now.

WORTHY WRAP-UP

1. Shopping for yourself is an investment in yourself. A Worthy Wardrobe signifies that you value yourself; therefore, others should too.
2. Settling is for dust, not your wardrobe. Buy it because you love it, not because it's on sale.

---

41 Luke 12:32 (NIV).

3. Style isn't about how expensive something is but about how well the wearer wears it. Your value is inherent and has nothing to do with the labels on the garment.

WORTHY WORDS

I deserve to have what I desire.

CHAPTER 12

INTENTIONAL INVESTING

Billionaire investor Warren Buffett advises, "Price is what you pay. Value is what you get." The same concept holds true when investing in a wardrobe. Price and value are *not* the same thing.

A $550 pair of designer heels are seen as a status symbol, but if they hurt so bad you can't walk to the front door, then those Satan Stilettos are of low value. But if you can wear those designer heels to work almost every day, then their value justifies the investment in price. On the flip side, a forty-five-dollar pair of nude pumps that you can spend all day in have a much higher value than a seventy-five-dollar pair of strappy sandals that match your bridesmaid's dress and that you'll never wear again.

Shopping for your wardrobe is about making intentional investments. While money is readily available to all of us, wisdom and discernment should always be used when shopping. Here are eight guidelines for making smart shopping decisions. The first four Fs apply to the garment itself, the other four are connected to you, the future wearer.

In order of priority, here's what to pay attention to for each item you purchase:

#1 FABRIC

This is the holy grail of quality. You should consider how a fabric feels (softness, sturdiness, scratchiness) and how it behaves (can you see through it, does it stretch, does it wrinkle easily?).

Silk, wool, cashmere, real leather, and suede are obvious examples of high quality. But it's not just about the type of fabric but also the amount of fabric used. While cotton is known to be a cheaper fabric, when a lot of it is used for a chunky cable knit sweater, then the value of the sweater increases.

#2 FINISHES

The divine is in the details. Check the inside of a garment for lining, pockets, heavy zippers, reinforced buttons, and snaps to hold in a bra strap. These details increase functionality, which then increases the value. Embellishments such as embroidery all over the garment and closely sewn together sequins also raise a garment's quality.

#3 FLATTER

It bears repeating that clothes are meant to highlight the great things about your figure (and yes, *your* figure has some great elements) and camouflage the areas that aren't so great. If you have a great rack, tastefully show it off with a V-neck blouse instead of hiding it under a layer of ruffles. If you've got a great ass-et, then a baggy pair of pants will make you look bigger than you really are. Instead, try a slimming flare or bootcut jean that balances your hips.

#4 FIT

It may surprise you that fit is at the end of the priority list, but assuming you can get the item over your head or hips, fit can be altered. If a pair of high-quality wool pants with a lining and pockets fit in the hips but gape at the waist, don't let an easy fix by your Fairy Godmother Tailor stop you from making that purchase. But if we're talking about polyester pants that are pulling across the front, then don't even bother. Walk away *immediately.*

Now let's talk about the garment in relation to you. *Only you* can answer these questions.

#5 FUN

Are you excited when you see yourself in that dress or is it just ho-hum? Ho-hum is not acceptable for *anything*, including your work staples. Even if something is a "basic foundation," like a black blazer or slacks, you should still feel amazing when you put it on. This doesn't mean everything you own is dripped in glitter. It's about this item "sparking joy"[42] and bringing a smile to your face.

---

42 Kondo, *Spark Joy.*

#6 (E)FFECT

What effect does this garment have? Does it send a message that is in alignment with how you want to be perceived? Are you comfortable with the kind of attention you will get in it? Every garment you own *must* accurately represent the woman you are *right now*. The size, the length, the color choice, the details, all these elements should be in alignment with the woman wearing them. Otherwise, you'll reek of insecurity, playing dress up in a costume meant for someone else.

#7 FUNCTION

What's the end use for the garment? What purpose does it serve and what hole does it fill in your closet? Does it work with other things you already own? Are those black pumps really *all* that different than the pair you already own?

#8 FREQUENCY

How often will you wear it? With most professional environments leaning toward business casual dress codes, most of your wardrobe should be worn in and out of the office. That means it's up to you to get creative in finding multiple ways and occasions for wearing each item in your closet. Pleated skirts are a wardrobe staple for me. For speaking engagements, I pair them with a blouse or thin sweater and heels or a statement boot. On the weekends, those same skirts get paired with a white tee shirt from Target, sneakers, and a jean jacket.

By keeping in mind these eight Fs, you're sure to make Warren Buffet-approved shopping decisions.

SPLURGE VERSUS SAVE

After working ten years at the headquarters of some of the world's largest clothing brands, I learned a lot about what items were high-markup items (beneficial to us, the brands) and low-markup items (beneficial to you, the consumer). Based on what I know about garment production and pricing, I've created some general guidelines about what items in your closet require a higher level of investment than others.

I call these "splurge" items not because I'm advocating silly impulse purchases but because you should spend on them the most your budget allows. Splurge items don't have to be high-end designer, but they do have to be well made. "Save" items are those you don't need the best your budget can afford, but they should still be of decent quality. No matter your budget, looking cheap is *not* an option.

> # I have standards I don't plan on lowering for anybody ... including myself.
>
> −ZENDAYA

Keep in mind that these are, of course, general guidelines for everyday work staples. Use discretion and the eight Fs when making exceptions.

SPLURGE ON PANTS. SAVE ON SKIRTS.

In general, pants take a factory more time and effort to make. The specifications must be exact, and the right cut makes a world of difference for a pair of pants. Fabric is also critical with pants, as you're looking for heavy fabrics, ideally with a lining, to hide any cellulite dimples or pulling across the crotch.

Skirts are usually easier to make (and easier to alter) and aren't worn as frequently as pants. The fabrics of my beloved pleated skirts are lighter, and therefore cheaper, than the sturdier fabrics of my favorite pants. As an avid skirt-wearer, I hunt the sales racks for skirts in all colors and cuts to add to my wardrobe.

SPLURGE ON BLAZERS & JACKETS. SAVE ON DRESSES.
Like pants, to be made well, blazers require great fabrics and lots of details. Tweeds, wool, and leather make for timeless options, but lighter fabrics can work as long as the blazer is lined. While sleeve length is an easy alteration, make sure the sleeves start at the end of your shoulder. You should be able to button or zip the jacket closed, even if you don't think you ever will.

For dresses, the silhouette is most important. As a pear shape, I know I need an A-line shape that's smaller up top with more room in the hips. Even then, I still usually need to get the bust taken in. For other body shapes, a sleek sheath with a straight, up and down cut, works wonders. Great dresses in forgiving fabrics and statement prints can be found at any price point, especially because you probably won't wear them as frequently as a blazer.

SPLURGE ON SWEATERS. SAVE ON BLOUSES AND TEE SHIRTS.

Thanks to growing up in Minnesota, I love a cozy sweater. I dress them up for big meetings or wear them around the house. The quality and appeal of a sweater is in the type of yarn and/or the amount of yarn used. Thin sweaters made of artificial yarns like acrylic and rayon look cheap and won't last long. But a thin sweater made from merino wool or cashmere feels amazing and will last forever if you take good care of it.

Blouses and tee shirts, on the other hand, are meant to be fun statement pieces in your wardrobe and don't need to last forever. Because I sweat a lot and because stains find me like moths to a flame, I refuse to spend a lot on my tops. At the start of each season, I stock up on my white tee shirts and button-downs at outlet malls. Polyester or cotton is fine here. But it's important not to have gapping at the bust or under the arms.

SPLURGE ON SHOES. SAVE ON BELTS, SCARVES, & SUNGLASSES.

My mother used to tell me, "You can tell everything you need to know about a man by looking at his shoes." I would say this applies to women as well. As grown women, none of us are allowed to have cheap looking shoes. Real leather (or high-quality synthetic leather if you don't want to wear animal products) and well-made soles are so important, not just because they look better but also because well-made shoes are infinitely more comfortable than cheap ones.

There's nothing sadder than seeing a woman hobble in shoes that hurt her feet. Again, this doesn't mean mortgaging the house for a pair of Red Bottoms. It's about investing in quality. This should go without saying, but when buying a pair of shoes, make sure you try *both* of them on. You have two feet, so you need to try on both shoes to determine if a pair works.

Belts, scarves, and sunglasses aren't wardrobe staples that you rely on every day. They're the panache that adds flavor, but not substance. Belts are great for cinching in your waist with a dress or adding a bit of a statement, but your pants should fit well enough that you don't need a belt to prevent the world from seeing your underwear.

Scarves are a nice extra layer that add color and softness to a look, but don't spend a ton because you probably won't wear them that much.

Sunglasses are the retail world's best friend, as they are *insanely* profitable for stores. They cost pennies to make, but thanks to them being a "status symbol," consumers pay hundreds of dollars for plastic. Don't fall for the trap. At least buy these items at a discount store or on sale.

SPLURGE ON WORK BAGS. SAVE ON EVENING BAGS.

Another reason Lauren's Louis Vuitton was a smart investment was that she'd carry it to work every day. It was functional and built to last. I tell women all the time that anything more than two bags when commuting to work is ridiculous. Whether it's your purse and a lunch bag, or a computer bag and your purse, don't let yourself become a Bag Lady.

Invest in a real leather bag large enough to carry your life: computer, wallet, notebook, makeup, and maybe an extra pair of shoes. Don't worry too much about the color, as you don't need it to "match" your outfit every day since it will probably end up in your desk drawer. Focus on quality and functionality.

I know I said there isn't anything sadder than a hobbling woman in heels, but the second saddest style violation is a woman carrying a ratty clutch or wallet to a cocktail or formal event. Make sure to have at least one go-to evening bag in a neutral satin or metallic that will go with all your dresses and that can hold your phone, lipstick, and keys. You don't need to spend a ton, but you do need one.

SPLURGE ON CLASSIC JEWELRY. SAVE ON COSTUME JEWELRY.
Gold hoops, diamond studs, pearls, watches, and bangles are all everyday jewelry staples that will never go out of style. Invest in the best you can afford in classic silhouettes that can be passed down to each generation.

I'm obsessed with costume jewelry. A statement necklace takes any blouse or sweater to the next level. A chandelier earring makes a white tee shirt an outfit. I own lots of the stuff but I never pay full price for anything.

Costume jewelry is another high-margin category for retailers: they jack the price up because they're betting on you to make an impulsive purchase. Instead of waiting until the last minute to shop for earrings for that gala, peruse the clearance jewelry section every time you walk into a store.

Don't overthink it. Costume jewelry is supposed to be fun, bold, and unique. Just keep it to one big piece per outfit and you're set.

SPLURGE ON BRAS AND SHAPEWEAR. SAVE ON PANTIES.

As we discussed in Chapter five, what's under your clothes is just as important as your clothes. No matter your bust size, investing in bras that fit and lift you comfortably are non-negotiable. Your back and shoulders will thank you. The same goes for whatever shapewear you choose to wear. High-quality garments that smooth and slim make any garment look more expensive on your body. Find what works for you, stock up, and take good care of them.

This may be controversial, but I don't care if your panties match your bra. All I care about is whether said panties can be seen through your clothes. Panty lines are sloppy and tacky. If you don't want to wear a thong, get a boy-short style that doesn't ride up, or layer them under some shapewear. Either way, invisibility is key.

My hope is these shopping suggestions encourage and empower you to wisely invest in your wardrobe. With each new, fun, and flattering item, you will quickly forget about and no longer "need" those old ho-hums cluttering your closet. Instead, each morning, you'll excitedly walk into a closet that signifies respect for your present self, the amazing woman you are.

But remember, this isn't about buying solely to accumulate more "stuff." Building a Worthy Wardrobe is about honoring your desires as well as your budget. By letting go of the past and making smart decisions in the present, you allow space for God to do Her part of providing overly abundant blessings.

WORTHY WRAP-UP
1. Be intentional, not impulsive, with your purchases.
2. Pay attention to the Fabric, Finishes, Flatter, and Fit of each garment. Consider the Fun, (E)ffect, Function, and Frequency as well.
3. God provides. Trust that you'll always have the money you need and the clothes you desire.

WORTHY WORDS
I am a worthy investment.

PART FOUR

POWERFUL

CHAPTER 13

THE POWER WITHIN

—

As I reflect on my own journey and the stories of the countless women I've encountered, I am in awe of how powerful we are, even when we don't realize it. There was power in my choice to walk away from the relationship and job that drained me. There was power in Stephanie accepting her body. There was power in Mrs. Rose letting go of those suits. There was power in Hannah choosing to put herself first.

> Our deepest fear is not that we are inadequate. Our deepest fear is that we are powerful beyond measure. It is our light, not our darkness that most frightens us. We ask ourselves, 'Who am I to be brilliant, gorgeous, talented, fabulous?' Actually, who are you not to be? You are a child of God. Your playing small does not serve the world.
>
> – MARIANNE WILLIAMSON[43]

---

43   Williamson, *A Return to Love: Reflections on the Principles of "A Course in Miracles*, 190.

Every minute of every day, we are given the power of choice. I hope that, by reading this book, you powerfully, enthusiastically, and consistently choose to love yourself more. And with this deeper sense of self-love and appreciation, you choose to dress a little (or *a lot*) better.

You can't have love without honesty, and building a Worthy Wardrobe is all about honest assessment. As you begin to curate your closet, there are three areas you need to be crystal clear about:

1. **Who You Are**
2. **What You Have**
3. **What You Need**

We'll briefly review each.

#1 GET CLEAR ON WHO YOU ARE

You're more than a wife, mother, daughter, sister, accountant, or volunteer. You're a splendid woman made up of a spirit, mind, and body. Honor all three as you remember:

YOU ARE GOLDEN AND DIVINE

Despite what life has thrown your way; you are a perfect child of God. You're on this earth because you have a purpose, and your presence has an impact on those around you.

Develop a spiritual practice that gets you closer to the Source Energy that governs everything. Spend a few minutes in meditation each morning; tell yourself "I love you" every time you walk past a mirror; discover what you're passionate about; and watch your entire life turn around.

Affirmations: *Today is the day I show up as my best self. I am golden. I am divine.*

YOU ARE PERFECT

Absolutely nothing is wrong with you or your body. Sure, some areas might need improvement, but those areas don't negate your inherent perfection. Be gentle with yourself and treat your body with respect—in thought, word, and deed.

Regardless of your size or shape, you're worthy of clothes that fit, flatter, and honor the woman you are right now. Do not beat yourself up while shopping. Finding what works is a challenge for everybody. A Fairy Godmother and the right undergarments make the process infinitely easier.

Affirmations: *I am perfect because God made me. Body, I appreciate you and I love you.*

YOU ARE PRETTY AND POWERFUL

Your purpose and your profession need you to look and feel your best. Investing in your image makes good business sense. Invest wisely in clothing, hair care, and makeup that makes you feel pretty. As you move up the ranks in your career, don't be afraid to be "appropriately authentic." Your confidence will inspire other women. Convey an "impression of increase" by wearing the styles, colors, and accessories that match your personality and help you stand out from the crowd.

Affirmations: *I am pretty, smart, and powerful. Investing in my pretty increases my power and influence.*

YOU ARE SEXY

Sex appeal is a state of mind, not a size or a body shape. Own your "Sexy Self-Mastery" by being unapologetically confident in who you are and what you have to offer. Have some fun exploring leather, lace, and even pompom socks.

Affirmation: *I am sexy and safe.*

#2 GET CLEAR ON WHAT YOU HAVE

It's time to come clean about everything in your closet(s).

LIVE IN THE PRESENT

Sever your attachment to the past, calm your anxiety about the future, and honor the present moment with your wardrobe. Shed the grave clothes that prevent you from living your best life now. Make your closet a sacred space so that getting dressed each morning is a relaxing experience. Have faith that just as God provided for your needs in the past, She will continue to do so.

Affirmation: *My closet is the perfect reflection of the woman I am.*

LET GO

Accept your perfect body just as it is. If an item doesn't fit or flatter, let it go. When your lifestyle changes, so should your wardrobe. Eliminate anything that doesn't have a purpose right now. Give yourself permission to express your personal style and tactfully reject anything you don't absolutely love. Be of service to those in need by donating your items to a meaningful cause. By clearing your closet out, you signal to God that you're ready to be amazed.

Affirmation: *I release all that no longer serves me, and I open myself up to new possibilities.*

#3. GET CLEAR ABOUT WHAT YOU NEED

Before you go shopping, remove any limiting beliefs around abundance and make smart shopping decisions.

STOP SETTLING

Show others how to respect you by respecting yourself and your wardrobe. Don't settle for anything you don't love, even if it's on sale. Avoid relying on labels or trends. You don't need anyone, any item, or any brand to validate you. Who you are is enough. Honor your desires and have faith that God will satisfy them.

Affirmation: *I deserve to have what I desire.*

INVEST INTENTIONALLY

No matter the price of an item, make sure it's of high value to you. Consider the eight Fs before swiping your card: Fabric, Finishes, Flatter, Fit, Fun, (E)ffect, Function, and Frequency. Use discernment when determining if an item is a smart splurge or save. You are your best investment.

Affirmation: *I am a worthy investment.*

The journey of life isn't easy. We've all had unique challenges and there are no easy answers to anything. But no matter your current lot in life, nothing is more exhausting and debilitating than being insecure in who you are.

Be grounded in the truth that you are divine and that you've made it this far. Be proud of your resilience and stop hiding your brilliance and beauty out of shame, regret, or fear.

Now more than ever, the world needs confident, inspired, and powerful women. It's time to step fully into who you are meant to be, live the life you're called to live, and do the work you're passionate about.

Will one great dress change the world? Nope. But the woman wearing it damn sure will.

Not only are you worthy of that dress, my friend, but you're worthy of having it *all*. You are worthy of being seen as the divine, pretty, powerful woman that you are while living a life beyond your wildest dreams.

You are worthy.
You are worthy.
You are worthy.

DO THIS FOR YOUR DAUGHTER

———

A couple of years ago, I had the opportunity to engage with a group of beautiful, bright, inquisitive middle-schoolers. During my time with them, I spoke about loving their bodies, no matter the current size of their jeans.

I wanted the girls to know a garment may not fit for many reasons and that *none* of those reasons have *anything* to do with their unique body shape or size. I pleaded with them not to take anything personally when it comes to shopping for clothes.

While I was speaking, I began to wonder how many women, especially those with daughters, know to not let the fashion industry influence their confidence. That realization fueled the writing of this book.

Whether we're mothers, aunts, sisters, teachers, or mentors, the young women in our lives are watching us. They notice how we talk about our bodies and how we choose (or don't choose) to invest in our image. As important as it is to *tell* these young ladies they are beautiful and worthy just as they are, it's even more important to *model* a belief system of self-love and acceptance.

> *Investing in how you dress and being courageous enough to stand in your beauty isn't selfish. It's an act of love that pays it forward to the next generation.*

As these young women are watching us, we should also be watching them. So many women I interviewed shared how they've been inspired by the confidence and unapologetic boldness of their daughters. "I love seeing her wear things I would never have been able to pull off at her age," Amy recalled; beaming with pride.

Maybe it's time we become the women we're raising our daughters to be.

I love you.

Yours in Style, Shopping, and Soul,

Morgan

SOURCES OF
INSPIRATION

———

Throughout my life, so many teachers have inspired me and changed the way I view the world. I truly believe that when the student is ready, the teacher (or book or video or class or church) appears.

These resources "found me" just when I needed them. The same will be true for you.

May this list be a blessing to you as it has been to me.

SPIRITUALITY
Discover the Power Within You: A Guide to the Unexplored Depths Within by Eric Butterworth

Maya Angelou and Oprah Winfrey both claim this book changed their perspectives on life and religion. It did the same for me.

The Principles of New Thought: Tracing Spiritual Truth from the Source to the Soul by April Moncrief

This book is part of New Member Orientation for my church. It's an easy read on how to go deeper within biblical teachings.

A Return to Love: Reflections on the Principles of a Course in Miracles by Marianne Williamson

Any book or any video by "Aunt" Marianne will open your heart, but this is her first and it is Oprah-approved. Her interpretations of God, love, and relationships will stick with you.

A Course in Miracles by Dr. Stephanie Schucman

This is a very big, very beautiful, and very deep book. There's theory that reads like a holy text and daily exercises to reflect on. I sometimes randomly select a page and the words are always exactly what I need. Reading *A Return to Love* first makes comprehending the principles in this book much easier.

You Are a Badass: How to Stop Doubting Your Greatness and Start Living an Awesome Life by Jen Sincero

Jen's style of making big concepts relatable makes this a fun and easy read. It will inspire you to own your inner Badass.

Radical Forgiveness: A Revolutionary Five-Stage Process to Heal Relationships, Let Go of Anger and Blame, and Find Peace in Any Situation by Colin Tipping

I learned the importance and practice of letting go by studying under Colin. The best part of this book is the incredible worksheet practice that I continue to use whenever I find myself upset.

Ask and It Is Given: Learning to Manifest Your Desires by Esther and Jerry Hicks

This book is good, but the videos of Esther channeling "Abraham," who is a spiritual being, are amazing. Search "Abraham Hicks" on YouTube and you'll get insightful guidance for any topic.

The Alchemist by Paulo Coelho

Profoundly simple, this fable tells the magical story of one boy's hunt for treasure and inner wisdom. Oprah and the entire world love this book. You will too.

WEALTH CONSCIOUSNESS
(Which Is Still Really All about Spirituality)

The Science of Getting Rich: Your Master Key to Success by Wallace D. Wattles

Short but powerful. Wallace strips away all the fluff to get right to the core of how to think differently about abundance.

Think and Grow Rich by Napoleon Hill

The inspirational stories included here prove that wealth is possible. I play the audio version in my car on repeat.

The Divine Law of Compensation: On Work, Money, and Miracles by Marianne Williamson

Another from "Aunt" Marianne. This one goes deep on how to view your job, your purpose, and your finances through a spiritual lens.

HEALTH AND WELLNESS
(Which Is Also about Spirituality)

You Can Heal Your Life by Louise Hay

This book will give you a greater appreciation for your body and how everything works together. "Great Aunt" Louise breaks down the emotional and spiritual meaning behind whatever "dis-ease" you're experiencing, as well as new thought patterns to help heal you. Whether it's indigestion, back pain, or acne, I refer to this simple guide for everything.

Sacred Woman: A Guide to Healing the Feminine Body, Mind, and Spirit by Queen Afua

I haven't yet read this, but my trusted Tribe highly suggested I add it to the list. These diet suggestions, detoxes, and meditations have helped my friends love and honor their bodies.

Becoming Supernatural: How Common People Are Doing the Uncommon by Dr. Joe Dispenza

Aunt Sine gave me a copy of this book and it's perfect for those of you who need scientific proof to support spiritual beliefs. Dr. Joe has studied lots of brain stuff and uses that research to provide tools to rewire your brain and change your life.

PROFESSIONAL DEVELOPMENT
(Which Requires Spirituality and Self-Awareness)

Executive Presence by Sylvia Ann Hewlett

This book magically combines research, professional advice, relatable stories, and tangible tips to help you increase your confidence and credibility. It should be required reading for everyone in business or sales.

Daring Greatly: How the Courage to Be Vulnerable Transforms the Way We Live, Love, Parent, and Lead by Brené Brown

If you haven't watched "Big Sister" Brené's Netflix special or her appearances on Oprah, do so immediately. And then read this (or any of her other books) on how to have the courage to show up in your life with grace instead of guilt.

Playing Big: Practical Wisdom for Women Who Want to Speak Up, Create, and Lead by Tara Mohr

I still refer to this book when sending an important email to make sure I'm "communicating with power." This features so many relatable examples from women in the workplace learning how to stop playing small.

BIOGRAPHIES

(Because No One Has Done Anything Great without a Strong Spirit)

Becoming by Michelle Obama

Mrs. Obama is the epitome of inspiration. I read this book in three nights because, each time I opened it, I felt like I was on her couch and she was talking directly to me.

The Surrender Experiment: My Journey into Life's Perfection by Michael A. Singer

"Cool Uncle" Michael has an incredible story of going from a grad student living alone in a cabin to leading a billion-dollar company. In this easy read, he proves that when you say yes to God, She always takes care of you.

Untamed by Glennon Doyle

The inside cover describes this book as "an intimate memoir and a galvanizing wake-up call." Glennon's honesty and ability to connect everyday life with deeper and bigger issues make me want to be a better writer. This book is funny and thought-provoking.

STYLE
(Because You Have to Get Dressed)

The Science of Sexy: Dress to Fit Your Unique Figure with the Style System That Works for Every Shape and Size by Bradley Bayou

Hands down, the best resource for how to dress every single body. Full disclosure: because forty-eight body types are featured in this book, only a few pages will resonate with you. This is more of a resource guide for folks in the industry, but it offers amazing advice and helpful illustrations.

A Handy Dandy Guide to Help You Finally Figure Out Which Body Shape You Are by Lisa Fogarty

The website sheknows (https://www.sheknows.com) does a beautiful job of breaking down the different body types, preventing the need to get out a measuring tape. It also provides flattering clothing suggestions for each shape and celebrities to use as muses.

The Truth About Style by Stacy London

I have seen every single episode of "What Not to Wear," the show Stacy co-hosted for ten years. Her career is what I aspire for myself. I love that this book provides Stacy's amazing advice as well as images and stories of everyday women getting styled and transformed.

ACKNOWLEDGMENTS

I write these acknowledgments in total awe of God's incredible greatness. As tears of gratitude fall from my eyes, I recognize that there has never been a moment in my life where the perfect people have not shown up at the perfect time to help me along my way. This book is no exception.

I am an example of what is possible when girls from the very beginning of their lives are loved and nurtured by people around them. I was surrounded by extraordinary women in my life who taught me about quiet strength and dignity.

–MICHELLE OBAMA

To my mom, Eileen, thank you for being my first and forever stylist and my first best friend. No dress is purchased or no decision is made without your influence. I love you more than words.

Thank you to each and every Aunt who has prayed for me and with me and has contributed to this book in a variety of ways. A special thank you to Aunt Gloria for being a trusted advisor and editor. Aunt Kay, your words of encouragement were always right on time. And to Fairy Godmother Aunt Sine, thank you for being a trailblazer.

I am an only child, but I have three sister-friends whom I love with every breath in my body. Camille, thank you for believing in the bigness of me for thirty-four years and counting. Lauren, thank you for being my mirror and constant source of inspiration. Jovian, your joy and faith are contagious. Thank you for encouraging me to always share my truth.

A special shout out to my My Tribe. These are the women I call on for business and life advice, for working meetings and cocktails, for soul circles and debauchery. Crystal, Shannon, Nicole, Margaret, Jovita, Kailei, Tiffany, Montrice, Liz, Elle Michelle, and countless others, thank you for your unique and lasting imprint on my life.

Immense gratitude to the place where everything started to make sense for me, Hillside International Truth Center, and to founding minister and my spiritual grandmother, Dr. Barbara Lewis King. Thank you for helping me discover the Truth of Who I Am.

A heartfelt thank you to every single client who has trusted me in her closet and to every woman who allowed me to interview her. This book would not have been possible without each and every one of you.

To my Worthy Wardrobe Community, it is an honor to spend every Monday night with you. Thank you for your honesty and commitment to this work. I am deeply appreciative of everyone who purchased this book before it became a reality. Thank you for your faith in me.

It's one thing to want to write a book. It's a whole other thing to actually do it. The structure and support provided by The Book Creator's Initiative was my saving grace. Professor Koester, thank you for my title and for telling me to "stop worrying and just trust the process." A special thank you to my publisher, New Degree Press. This is an amazing team, but a special shout out to my two incredible editors, Karina and Elina. Karina, your calm nature gave me a safe space to explore ideas. Elina, your impeccable attention to detail refined those ideas. Thank you for your dedication and pushing me to be better.

While this book is all about Girl Power, I owe so much to one very special man. To my dad, Robert, thank you for always claiming I was a writer, even when I insisted that "I had nothing good to say." Your prophecy has come true, and I hope I've made you proud. There is no love like yours, and I am forever grateful for it.

APPENDIX

———

Introduction

Cady, H. Emilie. *Lessons in Truth: A Course of Twelve Lessons in Practical Christianity*. Kansas City: Unity School of Christianity, 1919.

Chapter 1: My Story

Ackard, Diann M. and Carol B. Peterson. "Association between Puberty and Disordered Eating, Body Image, and Other Psychological Variables." *International Journal of Eating Disorders* 29, no. 2 (2001): 187-194.

Tiggemann, Marika and Catherine Lacey. "Shopping for Clothes: Body Satisfaction, Appearance Investment, and Functions of Clothing among Female Shoppers." *Body Image* 6, no. 4 (2009): 285-291.

Chapter 2: Golden

American Psychiatric Association. "Mental Health Disparities: Women's Mental Health." Accessed on January 11, 2020. https://www.psychiatry.org/psychiatrists/cultural-competency/education/mental-health-facts.

Cady, H. Emilie. *Lessons in Truth: A Course of Twelve Lessons in Practical Christianity.* Kansas City: Unity School of Christianity, 1919.

Cohen, Alan. *Dare to Be Yourself: How to Quit Being an Extra in Other Peoples Movies and Become the Star of Your Own.* New York: Ballentine Books, 1994.

Schucman, Dr. Stephanie. *A Course in Miracles: Combined Volume.* Mill Valley: The Foundation for Inner Peace, 2007.

Chapter 3: Foundation

Doyle, Glennon. *Untamed.* New York: The Dial Press, 2020.

Sincero, Jen. *You Are a Badass: How to Stop Doubting Your Greatness and Start Living an Awesome Life.* London: John Murray Learning, 2016.

Williamson, Marianne. *A Return to Love: Reflections on the Principles of a Course in Miracles.* San Francisco: HarperOne, 2009.

Chapter 4: Fairy Godmother

Attn. "One Size Fits None." December 26, 2019. Video, 4:06. https://www.facebook.com/watch/?v=1501521383348266.

Kapner, Suzanne. "It's Not You. Clothing Sizes Are Broken." *The Wall Street Journal.* December 16, 2019. https://www.wsj.com/articles/its-not-you-clothing-sizes-are-broken-11576501384.

Madden, Aemilia. "A Real Girl's Guide to Tailoring: What's Worth It (and What to Skip)." *Who What Wear.* October 25, 2018. https://www.whowhatwear.com/what-should-get-tailored/slide2.

Tabaka, Marla. "Most People Fail to Achieve Their New Year's Resolution. For Success, Choose a Word of the Year Instead," *Inc.,* January 7, 2019. https://www.inc.com/marla-tabaka/why-set-yourself-up-for-failure-ditch-new-years-resolution-do-this-instead.html.

Chapter 5: Body Love

Attn. "One Size Fits None." December 26, 2019. Video, 4:06. https://www.facebook.com/watch/?v=1501521383348266.

Chapter 6: Pink & Blue

Hewlett, Sylvia Ann. *Executive Presence: The Missing Link Between Merit and Success.* New York: Harper Business, 2014.

Howlett, Neil, Karen Pine, Ismail Orakçıoğlu, Ben Fletcher. "The Influence of Clothing on First Impressions." *Journal of Fashion Marketing and Management: An International Journal* 17, no. 1 (2013): 38-48.

Chapter 7: The Hero's Journey

Bellezza, Silvia, Francesca Gino, Anat Keinan. "The Red Sneakers Effect: Inferring Status and Competence from Signals of Nonconformity," *Journal of Consumer Research* 41, no. 1 (2014): 35-54.

Crown Coalition. "The Official Campaign of the CROWN Act." Accessed on May 17, 2020. https://www.thecrownact.com/.

Etcoff, Nancy L., Shannon Stock, Lauren E. Haley, Sarah A. Vickery, David M. House. "Cosmetics as a Feature of the Extended Human Phenotype: Modulation of the Perception of Biologically Important Facial Signals." *Plos* 6, no. 10 (2011).

Hutson, Matthew, Tori Rodriguez. "Dress for Success." *Scientific American Mind* 27, no. 1 (2015): 13.

Thomas, Rachel, Marianne Cooper, PhD, Ellen Konar, PhD, Ali Bohrer, Ava Mohsenin, Lareina Yee, Alexis Krivkovich, Irvina Starikova, Jess Huang, Delia Zanoschi. "Women in the Workplace 2019," *Lean In*, (2019): 6. https://womenintheworkplace.com/?gclid=CjoKCQjw_absBRD1ARIsAO4_D3v_SPjAgxO-6ObJZpSnzwn10yr44MV8tzF5TXKxZwo3Bxjwf8eCE9p8aAt-kmEALw_wcB.

Wattles, Wallace D. *The Science of Getting Rich: Your Master Key to Success*. Blacksburg: Thrifty Books, 2009.

Chapter 8: Sexy

Ben-Ze'ev, Aaron. "What's More Important, Being Sexy or Being Beautiful?" *Psychology Today,* May 1, 2018. https://www.psychologytoday.com/us/blog/in-the-name-love/201805/whats-more-important-being-sexy-or-being-beautiful?eml.

Ben-Ze'ev, Aaron. *The Subtlety of Emotions*. Cambridge: MIT Press, 2000.

Biron, Bethany. "Beauty Has Blown up to Be a \$532 Billion Industry—and Analysts Say That These 4 Trends Will Make It Even Bigger." *Business Insider,* Jul 9, 2019. https://www.businessinsider.com/beauty-multibillion-industry-trends-future-2019-7.

Doyle, Glennon. *Love Warrior*. New York: Flatiron Books, 2017.

Sayej, Nadja. "'It's My Ass and My Instagram': Amber Rose Is Over Your Slut-Shaming," *Harper's Bazaar,* September 25, 2018. https://www.harpersbazaar.com/culture/features/a23357956/amber-rose-slutwalk-interview/.

Smith, Sharon G., Jieru Chen, Kathleen C. Basile, Leah K. Gilbert, Melissa T. Merrick, Nimesh Patel, Margie Walling, and Anurag Jain. (2017). "2010-2012 State Report." *The National Intimate Partner and Sexual Violence Survey*. Atlanta, GA: National Center for Injury Prevention and Control, Centers for Disease Control and Prevention, 2012. https://www.cdc.gov/violenceprevention/pdf/NISVS-StateReportBook.pdf.

Tsjeng, Zing. "Lizzo: 'I'm Not Trying to Sell You Me. I'm Trying to Sell You, You,'" *Vogue Britain,* November 9, 2019. https://www.vogue.co.uk/news/article/lizzo-british-vogue-interview.

Chapter 9: Let Go

Weinswig, Deborah. "Millennials Go Minimal: The Decluttering Lifestyle Trend That Is Taking Over." *Forbes,* Sep 7, 2016. https://www.forbes.com/sites/deborahweinswig/2016/09/07/millennials-go-minimal-the-decluttering-lifestyle-trend-that-is-taking-over/#656b9d133755.

Chapter 10: Cleaning Out the Closet

Kondo, Marie. *Spark Joy: An Illustrated Master Class on the Art of Organizing and Tidying Up.* New York: Random House, 2015.

Rozenberg, John. "Clearing Clutter – Beyond the Closet." *Spirit Walk* (blog). December 2, 2015. https://spiritwalkjourney.com/clearing-clutter/.

Chapter 11: Stop Settling

Coelho, Paulo. *The Alchemist.* New York: Harper Collins, 1993.

Chapter 12: Intentional Investing

Kondo, Marie. *Spark Joy: An Illustrated Master Class on the Art of Organizing and Tidying Up.* New York: Random House, 2015.

Chapter 13: The Power Within

Williamson, Marianne. *A Return to Love: Reflections on the Principles of a Course in Miracles.* San Francisco: HarperOne, 2009.

Made in the USA
Columbia, SC
28 October 2021